RylieCakes

Lick The Bowl, It's Gluten Free!

lick the bowl

RYLIECAKES ESSENTIAL GUIDE TO GLUTEN FREE BAKING

featuring 70 timeless & mouthwatering recipes

Photographs by Shivyon Mitchell

To My Oma and Opa

You are the reason I wanted to be an entrepreneur.

You are the reason such fire and tenacity runs through my blood.

You've taught me to be humble, always hungry, and to never stop trying.

Thank you for always being my greatest fans and most honest critics.

I love you more than you'll ever know.

contents

THE BEGINNING

The original RylieCakes was not a blog, or a cookbook, or a collection of gluten free flour blends but instead was a traditional, brick-and-mortar bakery. Four walls, no windows, AC, or heat in the kitchen, early mornings, late nights, long days, a constant hustle and bustle of timers going off, cookies coming out of the oven and breads going in, soups being put out for the 11 AM lunch rush, and custom cakes being meticulously handcrafted morning, noon, and night for truly eager customers. The first RylieCakes was a huge, magical stepping-stone that brought me here to you.

After hundreds of conversations and commiserating with my customers over the challenges of gluten free baking, I knew they desperately longed for ways to make the process easier and more accesible at home. They were tired of buying 30 different kinds of flours in order to create eight different blends, only to use a cup here and there in a few recipes. Okay, perhaps a *bit* of an exaggeration but y'all know what I'm talking about!

And if you're anything like me, after ruining hundreds of recipes - eating cookies that tasted like cardboard, making brownies that had the consistency of tar, or baking cakes that instantly deflated - you ended up not using all the flours before they expired anyways. They were thrown away and the whole circus started all over again.

Needless to say, gluten free baking has traditionally been an ordeal for most of us - whether it's been tracking down all the necessary flours, creating homemade blends, spending more than our budgets allowed, wasting more ingredients than we'd ever imagine, or just the actual baking part of it all; the struggle was real and I was so over it.

Cue the development of my own flour blends. I wanted delicious, mouthwatering gluten free food and damn did I - and every other Celiac out there - deserve it!

I spent five years tweaking my flour blends and testing my recipes at RylieCakes Bakery. Lucky for me, I had an abundance of loyal customers and plenty of sporadic patrons that were always willing to provide input on their favorite treats: what they loved, what they cared less for, and what they really wished they could still eat after going gluten free.

They were not only my inspiration throughout the years, but also my official taste testers. Though I didn't know it at the time, the conversations I enjoyed with each and every one of them guided me here, to you and this cookbook. They encouraged me time and time again to share my passion for gluten free baking and cooking with the world. Though I cannot name all of our truly tremendous customers here, you know who you are; thank you from the bottom of my heart for being on this journey with me from day one.

I suppose that brings us here, to today. What a glorious day and a pleasure to meet you! Given the opportunity, I would hug you if we were meeting in person and ask you all about your love for baking... but since I can't, air hugs are coming your way! And I will do my best to share my never-ending love for baking, cooking, being kind, and eating throughout the rest of this book with you.

I was diagnosed with Celiac Disease in 2010. After false negative blood test results, which is quite rare as I understand, I went on to get an endoscopy which confirmed I was Celiac. The funny thing is, I had already been eating gluten free for nearly four years at that point. I had several other medical conditions I was dealing with at the time and eating gluten free just made me feel better, so naturally, I did it.

When looking for solutions to my many health issues, I saw countless doctors from 2006 to 2010, many of which questioned my diet choices. They said I didn't have to eat gluten free if I wasn't Celiac. So, that's when I decided to get tested. The only problem was, in order to take the blood test, you're required to eat a whole lot of gluten.

I ate gluten for two extremely long, miserable weeks; each filled with vomiting, diarrhea, fatigue, belching, flatulence, itching, cramping, aching, hot flashes, and everything else that I had stopped eating gluten to avoid in the first place! All of this to prove I had Celiac to a few skeptical doctors.

If you have Celiac or any allergy or intolerance, I am sure you have felt this way at some point in time. Maybe not to such extremes or perhaps far worse, whatever your story, I am truly sorry for your heartache and pains. I know firsthand how difficult it can be.

Despite all we have been through on our own, I am totally jazzed that we are together now. I am thrilled to tackle gluten free baking and cooking with you and I am beyond excited to share my rich, delicious, and mouthwatering recipes.

Eating gluten free does not have to be boring, bland, or limiting. It does not have to break the bank every time you go grocery shopping nor does it have to make you feel like an outsider. Being gluten free is an adventurous lifestyle that allows us to take chances in the kitchen, be creative, learn something new everyday, and grow as individuals. I am here to help you make it tasty, exhilarating, rewarding, worth every single dime, and every darn calorie!

I am *not* here to educate you on what Celiac Disease is or the science behind it nor to diagnose you with an allergy or intolerance. I will, however, give a quick shout out to why gluten is so important in baking. And therefore, why I've logged the man-hours to bring you fantastic, unfussy gluten free flour blends.

Here we go with just the basics…

Gluten is a protein made up of glutenin and gliadin. It is found in wheat, rye, barley, triticale, and various other grains. Appropriately, it does exactly as it sounds: gluten is the "glue" that holds together baked goods. When gluten is mixed with liquid it forms a network of cross-linked chemical bonds, which creates elasticity in dough. When dough rises, either while proofing and/or baking, this network traps gases, which allows the dough to stretch and expand. This stretched out gluten network is what makes bread so chewy, airy, and well, let's be real, delicious! Lastly, gluten is also great at absorbing and retaining moisture, allowing baked goods to stay moist longer.

This is why gluten free baking requires that we take our culinary skills to a whole new level. We must think outside the box to replace gluten; we must get creative, use different ingredients, and try new combinations in order to get the results we want. And we need to work with different flour blends that enable us to get a moist crumb, chewy texture, crusty bread, light and airy cake, or a delightfully crisp on the outside yet doughy on the inside type of cookie. Luckily, RylieCakes flour mixes are here to take the guesswork out of gluten free baking for you.

You don't have to think about the science behind it all, you just need to get your hands on a bag of RylieCakes flour mixes (pg. #14) and get to baking one of your favorite recipes from this book – though I hope you have so many favorites that it is hard to choose!

As you continue to read this book and dive into the recipes, I hope your heart is filled with joy and laughter. I am a firm believer that anyone can bake, so I designed each recipe with the home baker in mind; most of the recipes are easy, some challenging, but all of them result in undeniably scrumptious sweet treats that are sure to knock your socks off!

If you make a mistake, have a good laugh and then try again. I promise you, I have spent hours in the kitchen crying in the corner, licking out the bowl because the batter was so good but the final product looked like mush. I have even laughed so hard I peed my pants because working in a kitchen on your feet 12 hours a day has the tendency to make you delirious to the point that everything seems absolutely hysterical! Have fun with it - I sure do - and we definitely had a ball at RylieCakes Bakery.

One thing you will notice is that I did not include any prep times in this book. I have to be honest with you: I greatly dislike prep times. Everyone's style of cooking is so different and all of our skill levels are so varied. What might take me 10 minutes may take someone else 5 minutes or 20 minutes. Furthermore, all of our lives are totally, completely, 100% unique; though cooking in your house might be crazy and chaotic one day, the next it might be relaxing and therapeutic, who knows.

I beg of you to take your time with each recipe. Baking and cooking is all about the adventure – make sure you give yourself the time and energy to create a memorable experience in your kitchen. For me, it is turning on some country tunes (old and new, I appreciate them both), pulling out a bottle of wine, and throwing on some comfy clothes so I can bust a move at a second's notice. Do what suits you; make your kitchen your happy place.

I hope each and every recipe in this book brings you back to a great memory of a time when you loved to be in the kitchen - be it baking, cooking, or eating! I hope they make your heart smile and fill your home with insanely great aromas. I hope they inspire you to bake and cook more regularly.

May these recipes transform the way you live by creating a space where you can slow down and enjoy the little things in life. And lastly, may each one leave you and your family begging for more gluten free goodness!

Lick the Bowl – It's Gluten Free,

Tara Rylie

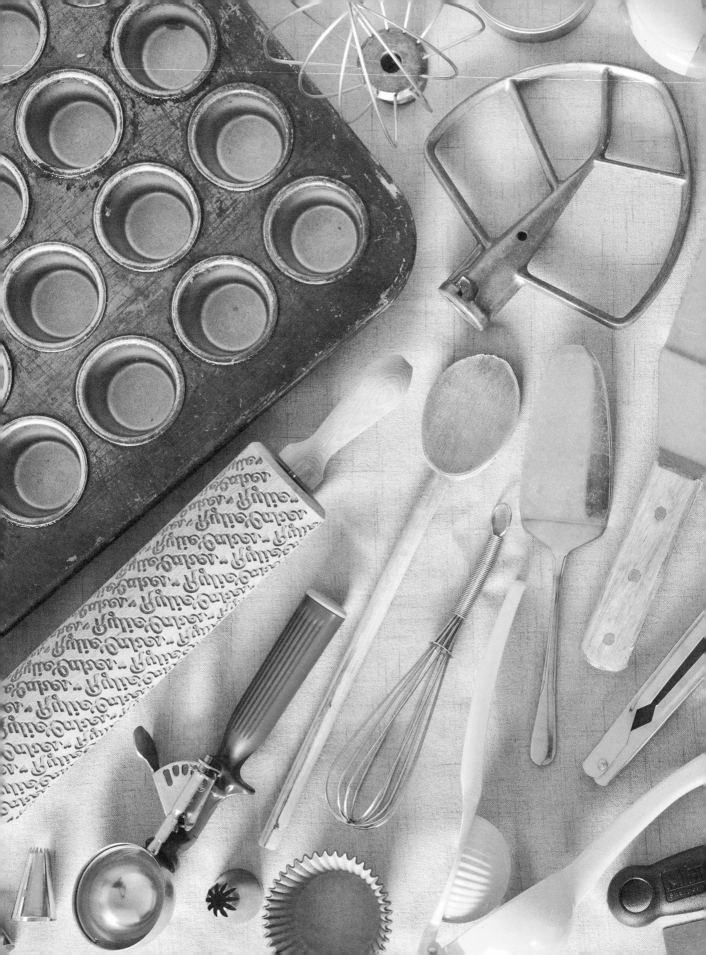

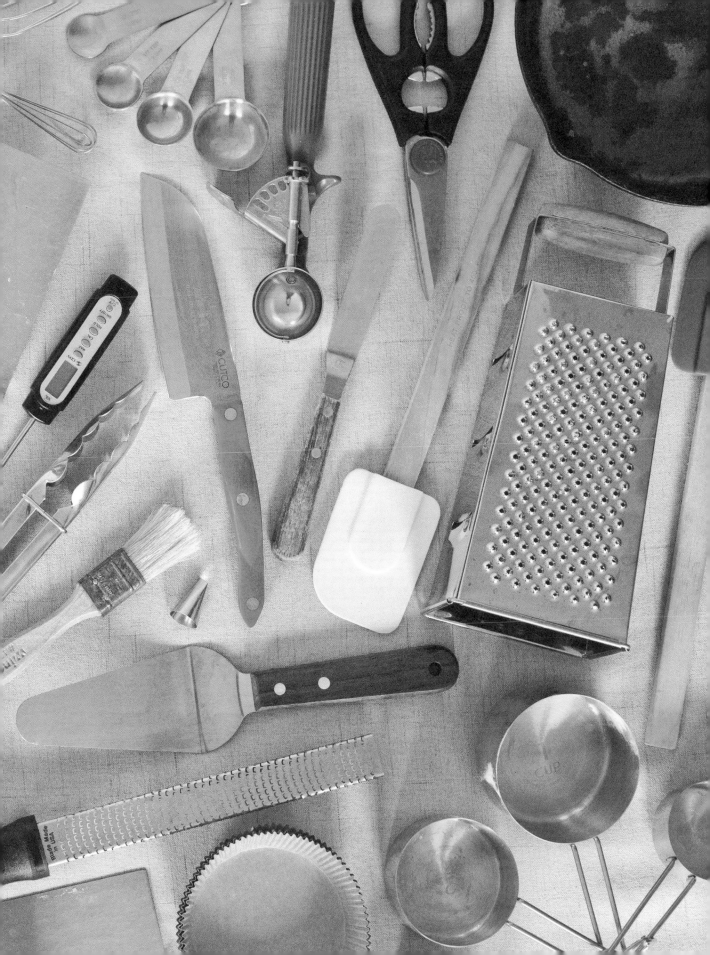

TIPS, TECHNIQUES, AND TOOLS

This cookbook is a blend of small-batch bakery techniques, combined with more common at-home baking tools, in the hopes of not only combining my two worlds, but also of simplifying yours.

Owning a bakery for the past five years meant I had the pleasure of figuring out the most efficient ways to whip up recipes and the best ways to train new employees to duplicate the process. During that time, I started to get a handle on what was truly important for every single recipe, what tidbits were more recipe-specific, and what tools I couldn't live without.

Before you move forward, I strongly encourage you to read through the following tips, techniques, and tools. Though you may have heard them all before or already own one of everything I'm about to recommend, I have found that revisiting the basics never gets old and only serves to improve your skills in the kitchen.

tips

TIP NO. 1: ALWAYS *MISE EN PLACE*

Mise en place isn't just about making a game plan; it is about meticulously preparing for the recipe ahead. It is about fully organizing all tools and measuring out all ingredients. This process creates a flawless routine that ensures perfect results every time. Once you *mise en place* enough, it becomes second nature and won't seem like a chore anymore.

So how does one *mise en place*? You simply put everything in its place! Make sure you read the recipe in full before you do anything. Then, measure out all of your ingredients and set them aside. Next, make sure you have all the tools you may need readily available: spatulas, whisks, extra bowls, baking sheets, muffin pans, and so on. And last but not least, read over the recipe one more time! And as you are reading through the recipe a second time, look at your laid out ingredients and tools to make sure you have everything you need ready to go.

TIP NO. 2: GO WITH THE FLOW

Baking has so many variables - think oven temperatures, baking times, the weather, and even the age of your ingredients - many of which we cannot change. So my advice to you is to just go with the flow!

My oven may be hotter than yours or your oven may have different hot spots than mine. If a recipe calls for 14 minutes of baking but when you pull your cookies out they definitely aren't done, don't be afraid to bake your cookies a little longer.

I live in Seattle, which means we usually have a lot of moisture in the air. You may laugh, but varying humidity really does affect your baking! Items such as flour and sugar can soak up moisture in the air. But on the other hand, the older your ingredients get, the more time they have had to dry out, and therefore will have less moisture than they originally did. This may cause your batter to be drier than you would have thought. Don't be afraid to adjust your batter slightly to accommodate your circumstances; add a smidgen more moisture, perhaps an extra yolk or a tablespoon of buttermilk when needed, or an additional tablespoon of flour if batter seems too wet - it's okay.

As much as baking is a science, it is also an experiment. I cannot emphasize this enough: don't be afraid to play around a little! The worst that can happen is whatever you're baking doesn't come out perfect, but I know it will still taste fantastic!

TIP NO. 3: BE CREATIVE + HAVE FUN

If you're not having fun, get out of the kitchen! I'm being totally serious.

Creating in the kitchen should be a magical experience filled with laughter, smiles, mistakes, wine, and plenty of snacks! So what if your cake is imperfect or some of your cookies have crunchier edges; all of these little flaws are what make your baked goods unique, homemade, and from the heart. Take joy in the process and that way – no matter what you make – the end results will provide sheer, unadulterated happiness.

TIP NO. 4: WEIGH YOUR INGREDIENTS

Baking is akin to chemistry, and, as with all science experiments, precision is the key to success. In order to achieve precision in baking, weighing your ingredients is a must. Weighing both wet and dry ingredients ensures consistently marvelous baked goods with each and every batch.

I understand not all home chefs are accustomed to weighing ingredients. I have also found that some of the smaller measurements do not need to be weighed, instead volume measurements do just fine. To account for this, I have used a combination of both ounces and teaspoons/tablespoons in this book. I believe this combines the best of both worlds, allowing for easy measurements throughout each recipe.

The best kitchen scales are those that can measure ounces and grams, are easy to read, and easy to clean. Great kitchen scales are affordable and easy to find nowadays as they are sold in most grocery stores and online.

Refer to Measurement Conversion Charts on page #18.

TIP NO. 5: READ THE RECIPE IN FULL BEFORE BEGINNING

I mentioned this in Tip No. 1: *Mise en Place* and I will mention it here again as its own tip because it is just that important. Please, I beg of you, read the FULL recipe before beginning! Even experienced, professional chefs do this. I even read recipes I've written myself and read 100 times before. When you are in a kitchen, life can start to happen pretty quickly; you're beating egg whites in one mixer while you have yolks going in another while you've got nuts toasting in the oven and… you get the point. If you read the recipe in advance and you know what step is coming next, you leave far less room for needless mistakes.

On a side note, be sure to pay attention to instructions in the ingredients list. For example, the ingredients list might say "10 oz heavy cream, whipped". However, as you're reading through the recipe, there is no step asking you to whip the cream; the recipe just assumes you have already whipped it. So when the recipe states to add the heavy cream, if you're adding a liquid rather than a whipped cream, you've got a big problem! One makes pastry soup and the other mousse. The devil is in the details.

I have used my best judgment as to when to include instructions in the ingredients list and when to incorporate them in to the recipe. In some recipes, I have done both, as I truly do not want you to miss that vital step.

TIP NO. 6: USE SAME TEMPERATURE INGREDIENTS

When baking, bring all refrigerated ingredients to room temperature before starting a recipe. When refrigerated ingredients - eggs, butter, buttermilk and so on - are room temperature, they more easily combine with one another and with dry ingredients. This small but meaningful step allows for

full emulsion of all ingredients when added to the batter.

TIP NO. 7: THE BEAUTY OF ICE BATHS

Ice baths are an easy and convenient way to cool down curds, mousse bases, jams, and sauces in a short period of time. They are quite simple to create: fill a large bowl with ice and place your hot saucepan directly on top of the ice. Then, stir your mousse, curd, jam, or sauce occasionally until cool.

If you don't have a proper amount of ice at home - I know this is a constant problem for me - simply place your hot pan on ice packs or even a bag of frozen peas with a kitchen towel wrapped around them. It isn't the fanciest solution, but it surely does the trick.

TIP NO. 8: WHAT DOES "QS" MEAN?

QS means Quantity Sufficient. It is a term I learned in culinary school and really just fell in love with. It means YOU get to choose how much you'd like of that ingredient, if any at all. So if you want to top off your muffins with oodles of sparkling sugar, go for it! Or maybe you want fewer sprinkles on your lava cakes, not a problem. QS is equivalent to "bakers' choice". Enjoy the freedom, be creative, and finish off each recipe just as you see fit.

TIP NO. 9: CONVECTION BAKE

When baking, I always have my oven on convection bake. It helps circulate the air in the oven so products bake evenly on all sides. That being said, I still rotate my pans halfway through baking as every oven has hot spots.

If you do not have the option to use convection bake, don't fret! Just note that baking times will vary slightly from those given in the recipes. Adjust as needed and you will be good to go.

TIP NO. 10: EGGS

Take eggs out ahead of time so that they are room temperature when you begin making your batter. When separating eggs, do so by hand. Separating eggs by hand is easy to do and makes it far easier to keep the yolk intact. If you break the yolk into the whites, start over! This could very well ruin your meringue as the fat in the yolk prevents the protein in the whites from forming foam. Lastly, add eggs one at a time to batter, mixing well after each addition. This process helps to thicken and emulsify the batter leading to perfectly chewy cookies and light, fluffy cakes.

techniques

CREAMING BUTTER

Whenever I hired someone new at RylieCakes, I always showed them how to cream butter and sugar. It may seem rudimentary, but knowing how to cream butter correctly is vital to any pastry chef's survival. Creaming butter in the world of pastries is equivalent to learning to crawl in the game of life. Once you learn to crawl, you can learn to walk, and then, eventually run... you get the point here. If you can cream butter properly, the world of pastries is your oyster.

The process of creaming butter incorporates air into your batter, which acts as a leavener when baking. Below are five simple steps to ensure your butter is creamed to perfection every time:

1. Make sure butter is room temperature - about 67°F.

2. Beat in stand mixer fitted with paddle attachment on medium speed for 1 to 2 minutes.

3. Scrape sides of bowl thoroughly.

4. Add sugar.

5. Beat for another 2 to 3 minutes until it is light and fluffy, approximately doubled in size. By "doubled in size" I mean you should visually be able to see the mixture grow up the sides of your bowl.

SCRAPE THE BOWL

In many of the recipes, you will see that I ask you to "scrape sides and bottom of bowl thoroughly" before moving on to the next step. I list this in the instructions over and over again because it is a commonly overlooked step that actually makes a huge difference in your end product.

Have you ever made a batch of cookies that spread unevenly? Or wondered why some of your cookies have crispy edges and others don't? Or have you made muffins where some of them rose to perfection and others just looked blah?

All of this has to do with creating a perfect, uniform batter. When you scrape the sides and bottom of your bowl throughout the mixing process, you are incorporating ingredients that often get stuck on the sides and therefore, never become thoroughly combined. Scraping the bowl is easy and quick to do, and turns your average baked goods into masterpieces.

ROTATE PANS 180°

Nearly every recipe in this cookbook asks you to rotate your pans halfway through baking. By this, I mean not only to rotate individual pans 180° but to swap pans' positions if you are baking with more than one pan at a time. By doing so, you will ensure even baking of all products no matter which side of the pan or which shelf in the oven they are on.

FOLDING, WHIPPING, WHISKING, AND BEATING

In the world of pastries, the following terms have implied meanings and also signify which tool to use. The following is just a quick cheat sheet to some common terminology.

Fold: To mix ingredients together with a <u>spatula</u> by scooping batter from the side of the bowl towards the bottom and then layering it on top of itself. Repeat this motion until ingredients are well combined.

Whip: Using a stand mixer fitted with <u>whisk attachment</u>, whip ingredients until well combined. Occasionally used interchangeably with *whisk*.

Whisk: Using a <u>hand whisk</u>, mix ingredients together until well combined. Typically used for all dry ingredients or all wet ingredients but not often the combination of both.

Beat: Using a stand mixer fitted with <u>paddle attachment</u>, beat ingredients until well combined.

IS IT DONE YET?

There are several techniques to tell whether a baked good is indeed done (e.g. the toothpick test) but the one I recommend most is to trust your senses.

Does it smell done? Does it look golden brown? Has it risen? Is the batter wiggly – meaning it jiggles and still looks wet? Or is the batter wobbly – meaning it sways together as one baked piece and will further set when cooling? Does your cake feel firm to touch and spring back or does the batter sink under your fingertips?

More often than not, people think too hard about whether their baked goods are done. Do yourself a favor, trust your senses!

RIBBON

There are very few recipes that call for ribboning in this book and that is precisely why I wanted to mention it here. It is not a technique I often used as a home chef so I figured I ought to explain it for those of you who want to give each and every recipe a whirl.

Ribboning means to whisk together egg yolks and sugar until they are so well combined that when you lift your whisk above the bowl, the yolk mixture falls over itself like a ribbon. This process can take some time - upwards of 10 minutes. So don't be concerned if your yolks aren't ribboning within the first few minutes, just keep whisking.

TEMPER

Tempering is the process of combining hot mixtures with room temperature mixtures. Whisked eggs or egg yolks are involved most often and the process of tempering is used to ensure the eggs are not cooked while combining.

To temper, slowly pour approximately half of the hot mixture from your saucepan into the room temperature mixture while constantly whisking the two to combine. The key here is to pour slowly and whisk quickly. Once half of the hot mixture has been combined with the room temperature mixture, place the saucepan back over recommended heat. Then, slowly pour the now-tempered mixture into the remaining hot one. Again, the key here is to pour slowly and whisk quickly. Once combined, continue to whisk and heat according to recipe.

INVERTING PANS

To remove cakes from pans, it is easiest to invert them. To do so, first run a knife along the edges of the pan to loosen the cake. Then place a wire rack over the top of the pan and while holding the rack flat to the pan, flip both simultaneously. Remove the pan and let the cake cool on rack to room temperature.

If the pan does not come up easily, lightly tap the pan to loosen the cake before pulling up. If the cake is still stuck, flip back to the original setting and use a small offset spatula to loosen it even more. Then, invert again.

LINING PANS

This is a little hack one of my employees taught me years ago and I still use it today. To easily line your square and rectangle cake pans with parchment, respectively place a square or rectangle sheet of parchment - slightly larger than your pan -

over your pan. Then while holding parchment tightly to top of pan, cut diagonally into all four corners, approximately 1.50–inches each. Press parchment into pan, folding triangle tabs created by cuts over each other to cover corners. And there you have it; a quick and easy technique that also allows baked goods to be removed from pans without a problem.

For circular cake pans, it is best to trace the cake pan on parchment paper and then cut out the circle to then place inside the pan. I like to make 20 to 30 cutouts at once so I can use them in the future as well.

tools

All tools in this section can be found on our website at www.ryliecakes.com/shop. If you do venture that way, thank you for supporting RylieCakes in more ways than one – it is sincerely appreciated. Most items can also be found in your local grocery store or bakery retailer.

PORTION SCOOPS

I understand portion scoops are not common in many households. However, they are 110% worth the investment if you plan to spend any time in the kitchen. Scoops are a standard measuring tool that are color coded across most major brands. For example, a blue scoop will always be 2 ounces or a grey scoop 4 ounces. This makes scoops quick and easy to use for portioning both sweet and savory batters and doughs. They provide consistency when portioning, helping to ensure your products bake evenly every time.

I use purple, black, blue, ivory, grey, and white scoops in this book. I have listed their respective ounce amounts as well as types of recipes they are used in, in a conversion table on page #18. If you do not have portion scoops nor want to buy any, that's totally okay! Each recipe states a yield and you can simply portion your batter/dough appropriately as you traditionally would have done.

DIGITAL SCALES

A digital scale is by far one of the best investments you'll make for your home kitchen. Baking is all about precision, and the best way to ensure accurate measurements is to weigh your ingredients. Weight measurements make for unfussy recipes that produce stunning results each and every time. Digital scales are affordable and easily found nowadays; it's a win-win.

THERMOMETERS

A few recipes in this book call for taking the temperature of cooked sugar. To do this, you will need a candy thermometer. A candy thermometer gets clipped to your pot before you start cooking and allows you to see the temperature of your sugar at all times. You can also use a digital thermometer if you have one, you will just need to check your mixture far more often than with a candy thermometer.

With that said, digital thermometers are great to have around regardless and I highly recommend every home chef have one. They are great for checking temperatures on meats, soups, sauces, and more. In this book, a digital thermometer will be needed for a few recipes as well.

OFFSET SPATULAS

Small and large offset spatulas are great for spreading batters, frostings, and fillings and I refer to them often throughout the book. They also work perfectly for decorating cakes and for use in savory applications. The best part about offset spatulas is that you don't need a million; not even a dozen! In fact, I only have two small offset spatulas and one large. That's it, that's all you need!

SILICON PASTRY BRUSH

I am a huge fan of silicon pastry brushes. A big reason for this is that they are way easier to clean than traditional brushes. Silicon pastry brushes can be ran through the dishwasher and, therefore, never hold on to excess oils like traditional brushes so often do. This advantage makes them far better suited for sensitive techniques like cooking sugar or for sticky situations like applying melted butter to soft dough. Additionally, being able to wash these so thoroughly helps eliminate any chance of cross contamination.

SILICON BAKING MATS

Silicon baking mats have become far more mainstream in the past few years and there is a good reason for that: they are so practical. Silicon baking mats do not crisp the bottom of baked goods nearly as much as parchment and they allow items such as cookies to spread more than they normally would on parchment. They also do a fantastic job of replacing foil in many applications. Plus, they are easy to clean.

I do not use silicon baking mats for everything though, as parchment and foil still serve their unique purposes. I specify either silicon baking mats, parchment, or foil in all recipes. If you choose to use a different option than what is recommended, it's no big deal; simply keep in mind that the baking time will be impacted and the end product may turn out slightly different as well.

OTHER LINERS

I prefer to use tulip muffin cups for my muffins. I have found that these liners are not only darling, but also give muffins a classier, high-end bakery vibe. Tulip liners are easily found online and in several specialty retailers.

On that same note, one of the recipes in this book calls for crumbcake liners. These specialty liners can also be found online and definitely kick your baked goods up a notch!

PANS

The following baking pans are needed to create every recipe in this book:

Three 6-inch cake pans

One or two standard 12-cavity muffin pans

One or two 24-cavity mini muffin pans

Two rimmed half-sheet pans

One 9.50-inch angel food cake pan (tube cake pan)

One Vintage Star Bundt pan or any shape 10-cup Bundt pan

One 9.50-inch glass pie pan

One 8-cavity mini loaf pan

One 12-cup Bundt pan

One or two 8-inch square cake pans

One 9-by-13-inch cake pan

One or two 6-cavity bundtlette cake pans

One 9-inch springform pan paired with one large roasting pan

Two 7-inch square cake rings (optional)

INGREDIENTS

FLOUR BLENDS

As you've probably already guessed, all recipes in this book call for RylieCakes Flour Blends. And if you've done your reading, you know that these flour blends have been tinkered with and tested for five years at RylieCakes Bakery. They are tried and true – along with each recipe – and ready to go home with you!

In this book, you will use RylieCakes Cake Mix, Roux Mix, Vegan Cookie Mix, Shortbread Mix, and Pancake Mix. To get your hands on these one-of-a-kind gluten free flour mixes, order at www.ryliecakes.com/shop or give us a call today at (206) 380-3414.

ALLERGIES

Allergies are so important that you will find this information not only here but in the Allergy Guide (pg. #17) as well. All recipes in this book are labeled for the eight major allergens. HOWEVER, they are labeled based off the ingredients in the brands I use. That being said, please, please, please read the ingredient lists for the brands you are using! Quick example, many major brands of butterscotch chips contain soy, there are a few that don't. Read ingredient lists carefully and watch out for any allergies you may have.

If you would like to see products that I recommend, head over to www.ryliecakes.com/shop.

COCOA POWDER

I almost always use Saco® Premium Cocoa, a blend of natural and dutched cocoa. It lends such a rich chocolate flavor to your baked goods. My mom used it growing up and I've never outgrown it. However, any premium, **unsweetened** cocoa will do for these recipes.

ESSENTIAL OILS

Where do I even start? Essential oils are part of my every day life – I use them for headaches, tummy aches, colds, stuffed sinuses, stress, anxiety, relaxing, feeling happy, as sleeping aides, and of course, in baking. They work extremely well when it comes to flavoring cakes and frostings; plus, they are all natural! But, never underestimate the power (and flavor) of essential oils. Make sure you add oils slowly because they can overpower any recipe very quickly.

CINNAMON

Whenever cinnamon is used in these recipes, I am using Saigon Cinnamon. I LOVE SAIGON CINNAMON. It adds an intense sweet and spicy flavor profile that I find cannot be duplicated by your run of the mill cinnamon. It is out of this world! If you're super into it, order whole sticks and grind them up in a coffee grinder when you need a teaspoon or two for a recipe. If you're a little more laid back like me, use pre-ground Saigon Cinnamon. It is easy to find and totally worth the extra cost.

HEAVY CREAM

This question always comes up: What's the difference between whipping cream and heavy whipping cream? It's the percentage of milk fat. Heavy whipping cream has 36% milk fat compared to whipping cream, which only has 30%. The higher fat percentage of heavy whipping cream allows it to whip better and hold its shape longer. Whenever a recipe calls for heavy cream in this book, I am using heavy whipping cream.

GELATIN

I very much prefer sheet gelatin, also known as leaf gelatin, over powdered gelatin. The benefits of sheet gelatin are significant. Sheet gelatin appears clearer in the end product, is essentially tasteless, easier to use, and leaves no chance of undissolved granules.

To "bloom" gelatin means to soak it in cold water for approximately 10 minutes in order to soften the sheets. Be sure to squeeze out all of the excess liquid in sheets before adding to recipe.

If you are new to sheet gelatin, the conversion works as follows:

1 envelope (0.25 oz) powdered gelatin = 1 Tbsp powdered gelatin = 3 sheets leaf gelatin

BUTTER

Always use **unsalted** butter when making the recipes in this book. In addition to that, I recommend buying a local, high-quality butter whenever possible as butter hugely contributes to the flavor of all baked goods.

EGGS

At home I use fresh eggs from our chickens. They are fantastic and we are totally spoiled! If you have access to fresh eggs, use them. If you don't, no big deal at all – just make sure you are buying large eggs at the grocery store. Every time eggs are mentioned in this book, I am referring to large eggs.

CHOCOLATE CHIPS

I love Guittard® Chocolate Chips; in fact, they are all we used at the bakery. They are high quality chips and are worth every penny. Their semi-sweet, dark, milk, and butterscotch chips are all peanut free, nut free, gluten free, and soy free. Plus, they are all non-GMO and use real vanilla.

ALLERGEN FREE COOKING SPRAY

To make things easy at the bakery, we always used Vegalene® – an allergen free cooking spray. To this day, I still use it at home. I love never having to worry about something so simple when having guests over; whether they are soy free, gluten free, peanut free or dairy free, allergen free cooking spray ensures I keep them safe when cooking.

DECORATING SUGAR

Many recipes in this book call for Demerara Sugar or Sparkling Sugar. I am a huge fan of India Tree products. They offer high quality products that are well marked with all eight major allergens. Plus, for me here in Seattle, they are local which is always a plus.

BROWN SUGAR

Whenever brown sugar is called for in this book, I am using golden brown sugar. I love the light caramel flavor golden brown sugar creates when baking. However, this is just a personal preference. Dark brown sugar will also work well with each recipe, but will give baked goods a more intense, molasses flavor.

VANILLA BEAN PASTE

Vanilla bean paste has an undeniably rich flavor. It contains seeds from actual vanilla pods, which gives it an intense vanilla flavor without the hassel of finding and cleaning pods. Vanilla bean paste can be found in most grocery stores or online. Vanilla extract is a perfect 1-1 substitue for vanilla bean paste.

ALLERGY GUIDE

All recipes in this book are labeled for the eight major allergens, plus sugar. If you see one or more of these symbols on the recipe you are making, that means the recipe CONTAINS those major allergen(s).

Contains Dairy

Contains Egg(s)

Contains Sugar

Contains Tree Nuts

Contains Peanuts

Contains Shellfish

Contains Soy

Contains Fish

Please note that recipes are labeled based off the ingredients in the products I use. That being said, please, please, please read the ingredient lists for the products you choose to use, every brand is different.

If you would like to see products and brands I recommend, please visit www.ryliecakes.com/shop.

You may also see this symbol which indicates that the recipe you are making is vegan.

And just a friendly reminder, all recipes are 100% gluten free and therefore, wheat is not included in this guide.

CONVERSION CHARTS

VOLUME

CUP	TABLESPOON	TEASPOON	IMPERIAL	METRIC
1/16 c	1 Tbsp	3 tsp	1/2 oz	15 ml
1/8 c	2 Tbsp	6 tsp	1 oz	30 ml
1/4 c	4 Tbsp	12 tsp	2 oz	60 ml
1/3 c	5 Tbsp	15 tsp	3 oz	89 ml
1/2 c	8 Tbsp	24 tsp	4 oz	120 ml
2/3 c	11 Tbsp	33 tsp	5 oz	148 ml
3/4 c	12 Tbsp	36 tsp	6 oz	178 ml
1 c	16 Tbsp	48 tsp	8 oz	237 ml
2 c (I pint)	32 Tbsp	96 tsp	16 oz	474 ml
4 c (I quart)	64 Tbsp	192 tsp	32 oz	1 L

WEIGHT

IMPERIAL/U.S	METRIC
1/2 oz	14 g
1 oz	28 g
2 oz	57 g
4 oz (1/4 lb)	114 g
6 oz	170g
8 oz (1/2 lb)	227 g
12 oz (3/4 lb)	341 g
16 oz (1 lb)	454 g

SCOOPS

COLOR	OUNCES	USED FOR
Purple	3/4 oz	cookies, fillings, donut holes, + savory
Black	1 oz	cookies, fillings, + savory
Blue	2 oz	cupcakes + cookies
Ivory	3 oz	muffins
Grey	4 oz	lava cakes + muffins
White	5 1/3 oz	cakelettes + waffles

LENGTH

IMPERIAL/U.S.	METRIC
1/4 inch	6.35 mm
1/2 inch	1.27 cm
3/4 inch	1.90 cm
1 inch	2.54 cm
6 inches	15.24 cm
12 inches (1 ft)	30.48 cm

MIXER SPEEDS

MIXER SPEEDS	NUMBERS
Low	2
Medium-low	4
Medium	6
Medium-high	8
High	10

TEMPERATURE

FAHRENHEIT	CELSIUS	GAS MARK
250°F	120°C	(1/2)
275°F	135°C	1
300°F	150°C	2
325°F	165°C	3
350°F	180°C	4
375°F	190°C	5
400°F	205°C	6
425°F	220°C	7
450°F	230°C	8
475°F	245°C	9
500°F	260°C	10

cakes

CAKE ASSEMBLY

To decorate a cake, the following tools are mighty useful:

Revolving cake stand
Cardboard cake circle
Serrated knife
Small offset spatula
Large offset spatula
Bench scrapper
Pastry bags
Decorating tips

1. To begin, secure 7-inch cardboard cake circle to top of revolving cake stand by placing a smidgen of buttercream in between cake circle and stand.

2. Cut tops off of all three 6-inch cake layers with serrated knife so that they are flat. The easiest way to do this is to start on one side of a layer and make no more than a 1-inch cut towards center of the cake. Make sure you are cutting across top of the cake and not into the cake. Continue to make small cuts while rotating the cake. When you get back to where you began, cut through to center of the layer. The top should easily peel off. If layer isn't completely flat, don't sweat it, this is a tricky step to master. The cake is going to be great regardless!

3. Place one layer on cake circle and top with layer of frosting. Spread frosting out evenly with offset spatula; it is okay if some goes over the edge.

4. If you are going to be adding filling to your cake, make a small wall of frosting around the outer edge either with a small offset spatula or by piping a ring around the edge. Then fill center with jam, chocolate sauce, lemon curd, or whatever else floats your boat!

5. Place second layer on top of first and top with layer of frosting. Spread frosting out evenly with offset spatula; it is okay if some goes over the edge. Repeat step #4 if adding filling.

6. Place final layer on top of second, cut side down. Spread a thin layer of frosting over top and sides of cake. If you have frosting oozing out of middle layers, simply spread evenly around cake. This thin layer is called your "crumb coat".

7. Refrigerate or freeze cake for 20 minutes before decorating*.

8. Finish cake off by adding an extra layer of frosting around exterior with large offset spatula. Then you can use a bench scrapper to create flat edges, a small offset spatula to create a spiral effect or rustic look, or piping bags fitted with decorating tips to create a design all your own.

*If during any step you feel like frosting is getting too soft or cake just isn't stable enough to move on, simply place cake in refrigerator or freezer for 5 to 10 minutes and allow it to firm up. Then continue creating your masterpiece.

REMEMBER, IT'S THE THOUGHT THAT COUNTS.
The cake doesn't need to be perfect. it needs to be you!

CAKE MAGIC:
RYLIECAKES FAVORITE CAKE COMBINATIONS

Cake: No Matter the Question, Chocolate Cake is the Answer

Filling: Dougy's Coconut Pecan Filling

Frosting: The Only Swiss Meringue Buttercream You'll Ever Need
(flavored with cocoa powder)

Cake: Game Changing Vanilla Cake (flavored with lemon extract or oil)

Filling: Finger Lickin' Lemon Curd

Frosting: The Only Swiss Meringue Buttercream You'll Ever Need
(flavored with lemon zest)

Cake: "Home is Where the Heart Is" Hummingbird Cake

Filling: Fresh bananas or pineapple chunks

Frosting: Classic Cream Cheese Frosting

Cake: Rich Red Velvet Cake

Filling: Just A Minute Jam

Frosting: Classic Cream Cheese Frosting

Cake: Ben's Favorite Carrot Cake

Filling: Toasted, chopped walnuts

Frosting: Classic Cream Cheese Frosting (flavored with cocoa powder)

Cake: Game Changing Vanilla Cake
(add fresh blueberries, raspberries, and blackberries to batter)

Filling: Just A Minute Jam

Frosting: The Only Swiss Meringue Buttercream You'll Ever Need
(flavored with vanilla bean paste)

GAME CHANGING VANILLA CAKE

Yield: one 3-layer 6-inch cake
or 18 cupcakes

I remember the first time we made this exact vanilla cake in the bakery. I had just tweaked my Cake Mix yet another time and decided to do a trial run on this recipe. I figured if we could create the perfect vanilla cake recipe, the world would be our oyster.

So we whipped up this recipe and baked it at three different temperatures and two different times to ensure we covered every last detail. And there we had it, on take #4, the most perfect vanilla cake you have ever tried.

We took one bite, then another. Then pulled off another piece and again another! We ate the whole cake! No filling, no frosting, just cake. It. Was. Marvelous.

From there we added sprinkles, lemon zest, almond extract, fresh berries, graham cracker crumbs, cocoa nibs, Elderflower liqueur, and Champagne to name a few extras. This recipe opened us up to a world of possibilities; it was a game changer.

---

12 oz Cake Mix

1½ tsp baking powder

¼ tsp salt

4 oz butter, softened

9.30 oz sugar

2 eggs

1½ tsp vanilla extract

8 oz buttermilk

Preheat oven to 325°F. Coat three 6-inch round cake pans evenly with cooking spray and line with parchment*.

1. Sift Cake Mix, baking powder, and salt into medium bowl and whisk to combine. Set aside.

2. In stand mixer fitted with paddle attachment, cream butter and sugar until light and fluffy, approximately doubled in size.

3. Beat in eggs one at a time until incorporated. Add vanilla extract with last egg.

4. Alternately add dry ingredients and buttermilk in three steps to creamed butter (i.e. dry ingredients, buttermilk, dry ingredients), beating on low for 30 seconds after each addition.

5. Portion batter evenly into prepared cake pans, approximately 12 ounces per pan.

6. Bake for 28 minutes, rotating pans halfway through. Cakes are done when toothpick inserted into center comes out clean; a few clinging cake crumbs are okay.

7. Let cake cool completely before frosting.

*If baking cupcakes instead, place 18 cupcake liners into two standard 12-cup muffin pans. Portion batter evenly among liners; a blue scoop works perfect here. Bake for 18 minutes, rotating pans halfway through. Cupcakes are done when toothpick inserted into center comes out clean.

Note: Try adding 2 oz rainbow sprinkles to batter for an easy, fun spin on vanilla cake!

NO MATTER THE QUESTION, CHOCOLATE CAKE IS THE ANSWER

Yield: one 3-layer 6-inch cake
or 20 cupcakes

I. Love. Chocolate. I mean that's all a girl really needs to survive, right? Well, that, and a dog and a cat and a big mug of wine… Surely those few things alone could solve just about any problem!

And I can't think of any better way to eat chocolate than in the form of a rich and delicious, homemade cake filled with even more chocolate. It's simply heaven on earth. No further explanation needed. Happy baking and happy eating!

7.10 oz Cake Mix

2.50 oz cocoa powder

¾ tsp baking soda

¼ tsp baking powder

2.70 oz semi-sweet chocolate chips

5.40 oz butter, softened

10 oz sugar

3 eggs

2½ tsp vanilla extract

8 oz buttermilk

Preheat oven to 350°F. Coat three 6-inch round cake pans evenly with cooking spray and line with parchment*.

1. Sift together Cake Mix, cocoa powder, baking soda, and baking powder into medium bowl and whisk to combine. Stir in chocolate chips and set aside.

2. In stand mixer fitted with paddle attachment, cream butter and sugar until light and fluffy, approximately doubled in size.

3. Beat in eggs one at a time until incorporated. Add vanilla extract with last egg.

4. Alternately add dry ingredients and buttermilk in three steps to creamed butter (i.e. dry ingredients, buttermilk, dry ingredients), beating on low for 30 seconds after each addition.

5. Portion batter evenly into prepared cake pans, approximately 13.50 ounces per pan.

6. Bake for 32 minutes, rotating cake pans halfway through. Cakes are done when toothpick inserted into center comes out clean; a few clinging cake crumbs are okay.

7. Let cake cool completely before frosting.

*If baking cupcakes instead, place 20 cupcake liners into two standard 12-cup muffin pans. Portion batter evenly among liners; a blue scoop works perfect here. Bake for 18 minutes, rotating pans halfway through. Cupcakes are done when toothpick inserted into center comes out clean.

BEN'S FAVORITE CARROT CAKE

Yield: one 3-layer 6-inch cake + 6 cupcakes
or 24 cupcakes

When Ben and I first started dating, we were both in the beginning phases of starting our own businesses. Ben greatly benefited from this as he got to eat a little bit of just about everything I was recipe testing.

His favorite then, and still his favorite now, is my carrot cake paired with chocolate cream cheese frosting. Wanting to impress him, I baked Ben far too many carrot cakes to count, for ridiculous reasons nonetheless. Like, there's a football game on tonight, better bake a cake. Or it has been a week since we saw each other last, better bake a cake.

Now that I think about it, I'm laughing out loud at myself; I definitely overdid it! Seven years later though, he is still all mine and every now and then he puts in a request for the one and only carrot cake that swept him off his feet just years ago.

7.50 oz Roux Mix

5.30 oz Cake Mix

7.50 oz sugar

1.75 oz brown sugar

2 tsp baking powder

½ tsp baking soda

½ tsp salt

2 tsp cinnamon

¼ tsp ground ginger

¼ tsp nutmeg

2 eggs

6 oz canola oil

6 oz orange juice

4 oz sparkling water

16 oz carrots, shredded

2.75 oz golden raisins

2 oz shredded coconut

2 oz walnuts, roughly chopped

Preheat oven to 325°F. Coat three 6-inch round cake pans evenly with cooking spray and line with parchment*.

1. In large bowl, whisk together Roux Mix, Cake Mix, both sugars, baking powder, baking soda, salt, and all spices. Set aside.

2. In 1 quart measuring cup, whisk together eggs, canola oil, orange juice, and sparkling water.

3. Create well in dry ingredients and pour wet ingredients into it. Using spatula, fold batter until just combined. Some dry flour may still be present.

4. Fold in carrots, golden raisins, coconut, and chopped walnuts until just combined.

5. Portion batter evenly into prepared cake pans, approximately 16 ounces per pan.

6. Bake for 32 minutes, rotating pans halfway through. Cakes are done when a toothpick inserted into center comes out clean; a few clinging cake crumbs are okay.

7. Let cake cool completely before frosting.

*If baking cupcakes instead, place 24 cupcake liners into two standard 12-cup muffin pans. Portion batter evenly among liners; a blue scoop works perfect here. Bake for 22 minutes, rotating pans halfway through. Cupcakes are done when toothpick inserted into center comes out clean.

"HOME IS WHERE THE HEART IS" HUMMINGBIRD CAKE

Yield: one 3-layer 6-inch cake
or 18 cupcakes

Nearly seven months after opening the bakery, I flew down to North Carolina for Posterior Fossa Decompression surgery to alleviate symptoms from a Type 0 Chiari Malformation. Whoa, that was a mouthful! The story itself is beyond a mouthful – and totally worth a book of its own. So, I'll just skip to my point here.

Ben, my mom, dad, and brother all came down with me for the surgery. I wasn't able to fly for at least two weeks after the surgery so we decided to get a cabin deep in the woods to pass the time. It was our home away from home and it was simply magical being there all together, watching movies, building puzzles, and having more than a few ab-exercising laughs.

It was during our trip down to North Carolina that I discovered Hummingbird Cake. I wasn't able to eat it, per usual, as it was soaking in gluten but man did I crave it anyways. It seriously made me drool and all I was doing was looking at it! Shortly after getting back to work at the bakery, I decided it was time I made my own hummingbird cake. To date, this is by far one of my most favorite cakes – every bite of it reminds me of a time when my family dropped everything to be by my side and there's nothing sweeter than that.

---

6 oz pecans, divided

5.85 oz Cake Mix

1.90 oz Roux Mix

1½ tsp cinnamon

½ tsp baking soda

½ tsp baking powder

½ tsp salt

12 oz bananas

4.70 oz sugar

4.40 oz brown sugar

4 oz coconut oil, melted

2 eggs

8 oz can crushed pineapple, drained

½ tsp vanilla bean paste

Preheat oven to 375°F. Coat three 6-inch round cake pans evenly with cooking spray and line with parchment*.

1. Line rimmed baking sheet with parchment, place pecans in single layer on parchment. Bake in preheated oven for 5 to 7 minutes until golden brown and have a nutty fragrance. Remove from oven, cool completely, and then roughly chop.

2. Whisk together Cake Mix, Roux Mix, cinnamon, baking soda, baking powder, and salt in medium bowl. Set aside.

3. In bowl of stand mixer fitted with paddle attachment, beat bananas until they are thoroughly mashed. A few small chunks are okay but you want to avoid larger chunks here; mixture should look like banana soup.

4. Beating on medium-low speed, add both sugars until incorporated and then add coconut oil. Although coconut oil should be melted here, it should not be hot. Make sure coconut oil has had time to cool after melting.

5. Add eggs one at a time beating well after each addition.

6. Add crushed pineapple and vanilla bean paste, beat on low until batter is smooth.

7. Add dry ingredients and 2 ounces of chopped pecans; beat on low until just combined and there are no dry spots left.

8. Portion batter evenly into prepared cake pans, approximately 14 ounces per pan.

9. Bake for 24 minutes, rotating pans halfway through. Cakes are done when toothpick inserted into center comes out clean; a few clinging cake crumbs are okay. Let cake cool completely before frosting and topping with remaining chopped pecans.

*If baking cupcakes instead, place 18 cupcake liners into two standard 12-cup muffin pans. Portion batter evenly among liners; a blue scoop works perfect here. Bake for 18 minutes, rotating pans halfway through. Cupcakes are done when toothpick inserted into center comes out clean.

RICH RED VELVET CAKE

Yield: one 3-layer 6-inch cake
or 18 cupcakes

One of the most frequently asked questions at the bakery from customers was, "What's the difference between red velvet cake and chocolate cake?" Traditionally, the answer would be that red velvet cake has vinegar and buttermilk added to it, setting it apart from chocolate cake. However, at RylieCakes Bakery, we made knock-your-socks-off red velvet cake thanks to our secret ingredient... booze! Yes, you heard me, boooooooze!

Chambord, a French raspberry liqueur, is what made our Rich Red Velvet Cake unique. Each bite is devilishly good, inviting you take just one more. I guess it also doesn't hurt that the cake is finished off by the sweet, tangy taste of our homemade cream cheese frosting.

Make no mistake, this Rich Red Velvet is no chocolate cake; it is in a league of its own.

---

12 oz Cake Mix

1½ tsp baking powder

1½ Tbsp cocoa powder

¼ tsp salt

4 oz butter, softened

9.50 oz sugar

2 eggs

1½ tsp vanilla extract

8 oz buttermilk

1 Tbsp raspberry liqueur

QS red food coloring

Preheat oven to 325°F. Coat three 6-inch round cake pans evenly with cooking spray and line with parchment*.

1. Sift together Cake Mix, baking powder, cocoa powder, and salt into medium bowl and whisk to combine. Set aside.

2. In stand mixer fitted with paddle attachment, cream butter and sugar until light and fluffy, approximately doubled in size.

3. Beat in eggs one at a time until incorporated. Add vanilla extract with last egg.

4. Combine buttermilk, raspberry liqueur, and food coloring in a liquid measuring cup, stir well.

5. Alternately add dry ingredients and buttermilk mixture in three steps to creamed butter (i.e. dry ingredients, buttermilk, dry ingredients), beating on low for 30 seconds after each addition.

6. Portion batter evenly into prepared cake pans, approximately 12.50 ounces per pan.

7. Bake for 32 minutes, rotating pans halfway through. Cakes are done when toothpick inserted into center comes out clean; a few clinging cake crumbs are okay.

8. Let cake cool completely before frosting.

*If baking cupcakes instead, place 18 cupcake liners into two standard 12-cup muffin pans. Portion batter evenly among liners; a blue scoop works perfect here. Bake for 20 minutes, rotating pans halfway through. Cupcakes are done when toothpick inserted into center comes out clean.

Note: If you do not wish to use red food coloring, add 1 to 3 teaspoons of pure cherry or pomegranate concentrate for a rich red hue.

THE ONLY SWISS MERINGUE BUTTERCREAM YOU'LL EVER NEED

Yield: 3 pounds
(enough for one 3-layer 6-inch cake + cupcakes)

Let's be real, there are thousands of frosting recipes out there to choose from but all you really need is one. One simply fantastic, home run recipe. And lucky for you, the search is over, THIS IS IT!

At RylieCakes Bakery we used this Swiss Meringue Buttercream for nearly everything – going through at least 30 pounds a week. Really, it's that good! If you're wondering what makes it so special, let me fill you in.

First off, once you get the hang of cooking sugar, it is very easy to make and quite difficult to screw up. Secondly, you can flavor it a million different ways with zests, liqueurs, essential oils, purees, and powders. And last but not least, you can make it in bulk and freeze it for months. It magically whips right back to its buttery, fluffy, luscious self every single time. The only downfall I can truly think of, is that you'll want to eat the entire batch by the spoonful while doing your happy dance.

This isn't a beginner's recipe. If you don't get the sugar right the first time, don't fret. Shake it off, shout it out, and attempt it again! Once you get this recipe right, your life will never be the same.

QS lemon juice

24 oz butter

10 oz egg whites, room temperature

18.75 oz sugar

2 Tbsp vanilla extract

1 tsp salt

1. Moisten paper towel with lemon juice and wipe down inside of stand mixer, whisk attachment, hand whisk, and spatula. Set equipment aside.

2. Cut butter into ½-inch cubes and place in refrigerator. Butter should be cold when adding to meringue in step #5, however, it should not be rock hard!

3. Fill medium saucepan approximately 1-inch up sides with water and place on stove over low heat. Place egg whites and sugar in stand mixer bowl and set on top of saucepan. Turn heat to medium and gently whisk mixture until it reaches 160°F.

   If you do not have a candy thermometer, take two fingertips and dip them into the mixture. When you rub your fingertips together the mixture should be completely smooth meaning the sugar has dissolved. It will be hot to touch so be careful not to burn yourself.

4. With oven mitts, remove bowl from heat and place onto mixer stand. Whisk meringue on medium-high speed until it is thick and glossy. When mixing bowl feels neutral to touch, you can begin adding butter.

5. Begin adding butter cubes one at a time until they are all fully incorporated. If your butter cubes are too cold, simply smoosh them slightly between your fingers before adding to meringue. Do not add soft, room temperature butter to meringue and do not add butter if mixing bowl is still warm to touch; both of these will result in soupy, soft buttercream. After adding all butter, meringue will whip up into an insanely luscious, silky frosting.

6. Add vanilla extract, salt, and any other desired flavorings.

7. Swiss meringue buttercream can be used immediately, refrigerated until you are ready to use it, or kept frozen for cakes to come! If you refrigerate or freeze buttercream, be sure to bring it to room temperature before rewhipping*.

*To rewhip, bring buttercream to room temperature in bowl of your stand mixer. Next, whisk on medium-high speed until buttercream forms. Buttercream may look like its curdled and long gone during this process, however, just keep whipping. It will come back and taste as good as ever.

CLASSIC CREAM CHEESE FROSTING

Yield: 3 pounds (enough for one 3-layer 6-inch cake + cupcakes)

I've been teased a time or two for having too many best friends. Someone once told me you can only have one best friend, that's why he or she is the best. But, that's not how I look at it.

I believe life comes and goes in seasons. Each season we learn more about the world as we see it. We discover more about ourselves and who we truly are. We then get a chance to recreate who we want to be moving forward.

That being said, I have best friend(s) from every season - childhood, high school, college, and life as a young adult. Each one of these incredible humans holds a very special place in my heart. With each I share a unique and undescribable, lifelong bond.

So naturally, I contacted one of my best friends for help when I was having writer's block on this headnote. Our conversation went exactly like this:

Me: I don't know what to say about my cream cheese frosting recipe! HELP!! Cream cheese frosting memories!

Kim: Oh my god! How do I even describe it?!? It's so f&*^%$! good!!! It's so good, you'll want to marry it and have cream cheese frosting babies with it! It's so good – I usually end up having it all over my face and in my hair! It's so good – if a glob of it fell on the floor I'd totally eat it. Cat hair and all. Now all I want is a bowl of your cream cheese frosting...

Those are Kim's words, not mine, but I think you get the gist. Make this frosting now and you'll have a new best friend for all the seasons of your life.

---

4 oz vegetable shortening

4 oz butter, softened

16 oz cream cheese, softened

1 Tbsp vanilla extract

1 tsp salt

1 lb 10 oz powdered sugar, sifted

1. In bowl of stand mixer fitted with paddle attachment, cream together shortening and butter until well combined and completely smooth. Scrape sides and bottom of bowl.

2. With mixer on medium speed, slowly add cream cheese to butter mixture. Once added, beat on high until mixture is completely smooth. You do not want any lumps of cream cheese remaining. Scrape sides and bottom of bowl.

3. Adjust mixer to low and add vanilla extract and salt. Continue beating on low while slowly adding in sifted powdered sugar. For thicker, more stable frosting, use all powdered sugar recommended. For looser frosting (not ideal for cake decorating but great for topping brownies), use less powdered sugar than stated in recipe.

4. Cream cheese frosting can be used immediately, refrigerated until you are ready to use it, or kept frozen for cakes to come! If you refrigerate or freeze frosting, be sure to bring it to room temperature before rewhipping*.

Note: Spectrum® organic, soy free shortening is available in most grocery stores. Look for it to make this recipe soy free.

*To rewhip, bring frosting to room temperature in bowl of stand mixer. Then beat with paddle attachment on medium-high speed until creamy frosting consistency is reached.

OUT-OF-THIS-WORLD SALTED CARAMEL SAUCE

Yield: 14 ounces creamy caramel sauce

Everyone had their favorite treat at RylieCakes, whether it was French Macarons, a Classic Chocolate Chip Cookie, or even a savory snack such as our Cheesy Bacon Bites. And then there were the salted caramel lovers...

They loved anything and everything with our homemade salted caramel sauce on it or in it. You couldn't blame them, the stuff was addictive! Arguably a sauce you'd like to bathe in. It was gooey like honey, buttery, rich, and finished off with a hint of sea salt. It was everything you could ever dream of and more.

I had many close friends and family members who could never, ever get enough this sauce. Whenever they came to the bakery, I would stop what I was doing and go fill them up a mini take home tub of our Out-Of-This-World Salted Caramel Sauce. I would then give them the old wink-wink and a head nod from the kitchen signaling for them to come back. After showering them in love, hugs, and appreciation, I'd hand over their very own mini tub of our heavenly sauce. Their excitement never got old and the memories of it made every batch a joy to whip up.

---

5 oz sugar

2.50 oz water

4 egg yolks

8 oz heavy cream, room temperature

¾ tsp sea salt

1 tsp vanilla bean paste

1. Cook sugar and water in medium heavy-bottomed saucepan over medium–low heat until mixture turns an amber color. Using silicon brush, occasionally wipe down sides of pan with clean water to prevent sugar from cooking to sides.

   This process takes approximately 20 minutes. Sugar may brown faster on one side of pan than the other – be sure to rotate pan or tilt slightly to move sugar around if this happens. Do not stir sugar! Such agitation could cause crystallization.

2. While sugar is cooking, ribbon* yolks in 4 quart bowl until thick and pale yellow in color; takes approximately 10 minutes. Do not use stand mixer to ribbon yolks, caramel will not thicken as needed.

3. Once sugar has reached amber in color, remove from heat and whisk in heavy cream.

4. Turn heat down to low and place mixture back on stove. Whisk mixture constantly for approximately 4 minutes until entire mixture is about to boil over. WATCH CLOSELY, once it starts to boil, it doubles in size quickly!

5. Remove pan from heat again and temper* caramel with ribboned yolks. Place entire mixture back on stove, still over low heat, and stir continuously until caramel starts to lightly boil around edges.

6. Strain caramel into large bowl. Fold in sea salt and vanilla bean paste.

7. Let cool to room temperature, stirring occasionally to prevent a film from forming on top. To speed up this process, use an ice bath.

8. Once cool, transfer caramel to an airtight container and refrigerate overnight to set.

9. Caramel can be used as a filling in cakes and cupcakes, as frosting on brownies (pg. #94), or it can be reheated in microwave to drizzle over your favorite ice cream!

*See "tips, techniques, and tools" chapter on pg. #9-10 for instructions on how to ribbon and temper.

JUST A MINUTE JAM

Yield: 1 pound juicy jam
(enough for one 3-layer 6-inch cake, cupcakes, or plenty of toast)

I've always been a huge fan of jams, jellies, and the like. They pair well with just about anything – strawberry jam on a PB & J sandwich, peach preserves used to glaze pork chops, raspberry–jalapeno jelly on a turkey club, blueberry jam baked into a cheesecake, or a dollop of orange marmalade right in the center of a butter thumbprint cookie. So when I learned in culinary school just how easy it was to make your own jams, jellies, preserves, and marmalades, I never stopped!

I make one batch weekly at our house, usually every Sunday. More often than not we roll with Raspberry Jam so that was my fruit of choice here. However, this exact recipe works great with blueberries, blackberries, and strawberries alike.

Enough said, let's get jammin'!

---

8 oz sugar

½ tsp powdered pectin

16 oz frozen raspberries

1 Tbsp fresh lemon juice

½ tsp lemon zest

1. In small bowl, whisk together sugar and pectin. Set aside.

2. Add frozen berries to medium saucepan and bring to a rolling boil over medium-high heat, stirring occasionally.

3. Once berries have reached a rolling boil, add sugar mixture, fresh lemon juice, and lemon zest and stir to combine.

4. Let jam boil for another 5 minutes. Be sure to stir occasionally with wooden spoon so that mixture does not stick to bottom of pan.

5. After 5 minutes, turn heat down as low as possible. Simmer jam for 10 minutes.

6. After 10 minutes, remove saucepan from heat and place on wire cooling rack. Let jam come to room temperature before transferring to an airtight container. Refrigerate overnight before using.

Note: If using strawberries in place of raspberries, I recommend cooking jam all the way through with whole strawberries. They will break down slightly when cooking. Then after removing jam from heat in step #6, pulse with immersion blender to break up strawberries to desired texture. I blend my strawberry jam until totally smooth – it is to die for!

ANYTHING GOES MOUSSE

Yield: 8 (3.50 ounce) luscious servings

Remember when I mentioned to always read the instructions within the ingredients? If not, back it up and read over the tips section on page #8. Here is a great example of what not to do.

When I was in culinary school I'd always go home and practice new recipes – I would even be a dare devil and jump ahead to recipes we hadn't yet covered. And that's how the Mousse Debacle of 2012 came to be. Mind you, I had never made mousse from scratch before.

To begin, I made a *pate a bombe* without struggle. Then I made a chocolate base and gently folded them together when their temperatures were just right; easy peasy lemon squeezy. Finally, I folded in the heavy cream and ended up with chocolate soup...

For the life of me I couldn't figure out where I had went wrong. I asked my friend to look over the recipe; perhaps she'd catch something I missed. Sure enough, she did. The recipe called for "12 oz heavy cream, whipped". I skipped over the most important word: whipped. And since there was no step to whip the cream in the directions, I completely missed it all together. This one mistake ruined my entire mousse.

Don't be like me and end up with soupy mousse. Take my tips to heart as I've already made the mistakes for you!

After the debacle, I found a mousse technique that skips over all those fancy processes we learned in culinary school and works for nearly any thickened sauce (hence, it's name). This Anything Goes Mousse is silky, rich, light as air, and will always leave you wanting more.

1.50 sheets gelatin

2 eggs

1 egg yolk

5.75 oz sugar

2.50 oz lava glaze (pg. #48)

3 oz butter, cut in ½" cubes

14 oz heavy cream, keep refrigerated until ready to use

1. Bloom gelatin sheets (pg. #14) in 1 quart liquid measuring cup filled with cold water. Be sure sheets are fully submerged in water; you can cut them in half to make them fit better if needed.

2. Fill medium saucepan approximately 1-inch up sides with water and place on stove over low heat.

3. In medium size bowl*, whisk together eggs, egg yolk, sugar, and lava glaze.

4. Place bowl on top of saucepan and turn heat up to medium. Cook for 15 minutes stirring continually with whisk until mixture thickens. If egg starts to cook on sides of bowl, slightly turn down heat**.

5. When mixture has thickened – has a firm flow to it – remove from heat. Immediately press gelatin (squeeze out all excess liquid) and add to mixture; whisk until gelatin completely dissolves.

6. Add butter and whisk until incorporated.

7. Set bowl of chocolate base on an ice bath and stir occasionally with spatula until chilled.

8. While chocolate base is cooling, whip heavy cream in bowl of stand mixer fitted with whisk attachment until stiff peaks form. Do not over whip.

9. Once chocolate base is thoroughly cooled and thickened, begin folding in whipped cream. Scoop one-third of whipped cream into base and fold until completely incorporated. This step is very important as it loosens the chocolate base without deflating all of the whipped cream.

10. Next, fold in half of remaining whipped cream. Be sure to fold underneath entire mixture as well as around edges of bowl – the less folding you can do while incorporating the two mixtures the better.

11. Lastly, fold in remaining whipped cream.

12. Mousse can be used in cakes and cupcakes right away or it can be piped into ramekins or stemless wine glasses to create darling mousse cups. Either way, be sure to let both cakes filled with mousse or mousse cups set in refrigerator overnight before serving.

Note: I recommend topping off mousse cups with dollops of whipped cream, a few fresh berries, and some hearty chocolate shavings.

*Make sure bowl sits on top of saucepan perfectly before going any further in recipe. The perfect fit will leave no air gaps for steam to escape; bowl will also not dip too far down into saucepan as to touch boiling water. Water baths gently heat mixture and therefore, gradually cooks mousse base.

**If cooked egg pieces exist in chocolate base, simply strain mixture into another bowl after removing from heat and before adding gelatin.

DOUGY'S COCONUT PECAN FILLING

Yield: 1 pound 12 ounces of the best filling this world has to offer
(enough for two 3-layer 6-inch cakes or oodles of cupcakes)

Every year for Christmas we used to have a family email thread that would go around asking what was on everyone's list – this included our immediate family, my Oma and Opa, my mom's sister, her husband, and her two kids. Some of our wishes were lofty: world peace, an A+ in Modern Algebra, and a solution to global warming. Other wishes were left simple: new clothes, framed family photos, or good books.

My dad's list was always simple and consistent. He desired to spend more time with family, go on more adventures together, and eat more RylieCakes. Last year, all he put on his list was a tub of my coconut pecan filling.

So on Christmas day as we all opened gifts, we passed around a tub of Dougy's Coconut Pecan Filling, each enjoying more than one heaping spoonful. Though this salty, sweet, creamy, and totally nutty filling is fantastic in cakes, all you really need is a (really big) spoon.

---

4 oz pecans

7 oz brown sugar

8 oz evaporated milk

3 egg yolks, lightly beaten

4 oz butter, cut into ½" cubes

1 tsp almond extract

¼ tsp salt

5.25 oz shredded coconut

Preheat oven to 375°F.

1. Line rimmed baking sheet with parchment, place pecans in single layer on parchment. Bake in preheated oven for 5 to 7 minutes until golden brown and have a nutty fragrance. Remove from oven, cool completely, and then finely chop.

2. In medium saucepan, combine brown sugar, evaporated milk, egg yolks, butter, almond extract, and salt. Cook over medium heat, whisking constantly.

3. When mixture begins to boil and thicken, remove from heat and stir in chopped pecans and shredded coconut.

4. Place pan on wire rack to cool. Let filling come to room temperature before using on a cake, in cupcakes, or eating by the spoonful!

5. Store filling in an airtight container in refrigerator.

FINGER LICKIN' LEMON CURD

Yield: 10 (4 ounce) finger-licking servings

Let me err on the side of caution here and say this recipe is for the more experienced or adventurous home chef.

If you are anything like me, you just read that and don't care! You are all over it with a "BRING IT ON!" kind of attitude. And if you are a little hesitant, that's okay too, you're not alone.

Over the years I have trained several people on how to make lemon curd and their first few batches were hardly ever consistent. First, the curd would turn out runny, more like lemony slime than custard. Then, it would be far too firm – more like lemon Play-doh®. After a few screwy batches, my employees would get the hang of it and create the most sensational lemon curd. It was sweet and creamy, rich and tangy, and oh-so-silky smooth.

Moral of the story: If you don't get this recipe right the first time (or ten), don't give up, you're not the only one. Practice makes perfect and once you nail it, you'll be scraping every last bit out of the bowl and begging for more!

---

2 sheets gelatin

4 eggs

5 egg yolks

16 oz sugar

10 oz fresh lemon juice

1 large lemon, zested

6 oz butter, cut into ½" cubes

1. Bloom gelatin sheets (pg. #14) in 1 quart liquid measuring cup filled with cold water. Be sure sheets are fully submerged in water; you can cut them in half to make them fit better if needed.

2. Fill medium saucepan approximately 1-inch up sides with water and place on stove over low heat.

3. In medium size bowl*, whisk together eggs, egg yolks, sugar, lemon juice, and lemon zest.

4. Place bowl on top of saucepan and turn heat up to medium. Cook for approximately 15 minutes stirring continually until mixture thickens. If egg starts to cook on sides of bowl, slightly turn heat down**.

5. When curd has thickened, remove from heat. Immediately press gelatin (squeeze out all excess liquid) and add to curd, whisk until gelatin completely dissolves.

6. Add butter and whisk until incorporated.

7. Let cool to room temperature and then transfer to an airtight container. Store curd in refrigerator overnight to set. Once set, use liberally in cakes and cupcakes, fold with whipped cream for a delightful mousse, or eat alone with some graham cracker crumbs sprinkled on top.

Note: Replace lemon juice and zest with fresh grapefruit juice and zest for another mind-blowing curd!

*Make sure bowl sits on top of saucepan perfectly before going any further in recipe. The perfect fit will leave no air gaps for steam to escape; bowl will also not dip too far down into saucepan as to touch the boiling water. Water baths gently heat mixture and therefore, gradually cooks curd.

**If cooked egg pieces exist in curd, strain mixture into another bowl after removing from heat and before adding gelatin.

THE SISTERS' LAVA CAKES

Yield: 12 scrumptious bundtlettes

One of my favorite days at the bakery every year was our anniversary. The first weekend of March we invited fans, friends, and family to come celebrate another year in business with us. We had fantastic sales, served sweet and savory bites on the hour every hour, raffled off prizes for free treats, and of course, blew out candles on a larger than life birthday cake! The very best part of it all was spending time with our customers who truly believed in us, day in and day out.

My Aunt Kim, Uncle Darrin, and their four kids were amongst our supporters and my cousins were perhaps some of the cutest faces to ever come through our doors. One year, as I was heading over to their table to spend some quality time with them, my little cousin Isabelle – better known as Belly – broke down crying.

Her face was smothered in chocolate sauce and teardrops. I hugged her into my lap and asked her what was going on. In between deep breaths of desperation and sheer sadness Belly said, "Natalie ate all of her lava cake… and I didn't get a bite." Natalie immediately shot back, "She had her own lava cake!!"

I'm quite certain this says it all: these lava cakes are not made for sharing and are definitely worth crying over.

Cake

9.25 oz Cake Mix

1.25 oz Roux Mix

½ tsp baking soda

½ tsp salt

8 oz butter

2 oz cocoa

6 oz water

15 oz sugar

8.50 oz sour cream

1 Tbsp vanilla extract

2 eggs, lightly beaten

Glaze

12 oz semi-sweet chocolate chips

6 oz heavy cream

2.85 oz corn syrup

1 tsp vanilla extract

QS chocolate sprinkles

Preheat oven to 325°F. Coat two bundtlette cake pans evenly with cooking spray and then dust both pans with a mixture of 2 Tbsp Roux Mix + 1 Tbsp cocoa powder.

Cake

1. In medium bowl, whisk together Cake Mix, Roux Mix, baking soda, and salt. Set aside.

2. Melt butter in large saucepan over medium-low heat. All ingredients will eventually be mixed into saucepan so it is important that it is much larger than only the butter's volume.

3. Once butter is melted, add cocoa powder and stir until smooth. Whisk in water and remove from heat.

4. Add sugar, sour cream, vanilla extract, and eggs to warm cocoa mixture. Whisk until smooth.

5. Add dry ingredients to cocoa mixture. Fold with spatula until well blended.

6. Portion batter evenly among all 12 cavities; a grey scoop works perfect here.

7. Bake for 16 minutes, rotating pans halfway through. After removing from oven, allow bundtlettes to cool in pans on wire rack for 25 minutes before inverting.

Glaze + Assembly

1. Place chocolate in large bowl, set aside.

2. Combine heavy cream, corn syrup, and vanilla extract in small saucepan over medium-high heat. Cook mixture, stirring occasionally, until it begins to boil. Pour hot cream mixture over chocolate and whisk until smooth.

3. Allow glaze to cool significantly before glazing lava cakes. While glaze is cooling, remove lava cakes from pan if you haven't already.

4. To glaze lava cakes, you can get fancy and place glaze in piping bag. Cut off tip of piping bag and then move your wrist in small zigzag motions around the lava cakes to create sophisticated designs.

   Or you can face the facts and realize that these scrumptious little gifts to the world will be in your tummy in no time and thus, you can use a spoon to drizzle (or drench) each cake with glaze. Either way, don't forget to top them off with oodles of chocolate sprinkles!

Note: This batter can sit in the refrigerator for up to four days. So if you only have one pan (makes 6) or just want to make a smaller batch, go ahead and store remaining batter in an airtight container until you are ready for more!

NY STYLE CHEESECAKE

Yield: 10 enormous slices

One freezing cold January my mom and I found ourselves in NYC for a weekend. We arrived late on a Friday night so decided to skip dinner and go straight to dessert. We bundled up head to toe with only our eyes revealed to brave the icy air and frigid wind blasts tunneling through the city blocks. We didn't even make it 20 feet from the hotel before we ran for our lives back indoors! So, we decided to order in instead.

Not growing up in a huge city, we were not used to such convenience so late at night. My mom and I were over the moon that we could get a whole cheesecake delivered right to our room at nearly midnight!

We immediately dug in. I only ate the filling off the top, trying to avoid the sponge cake crust and any cross contamination at all costs. Looking back I have to laugh at myself because nowadays you would never find me dancing with the devil like that! Never. EVER. However stupid my actions were then, they introduced me to the first cheesecake I ever truly loved and clearly, never forgot.

I wrote the following recipe based off what I could remember from that late, chilly city night, curled up in a hotel bed with my mom and an entire cheesecake just for two. It is not a beginner's recipe but don't let it intimidate you. Read the recipe before you begin, *mise en place*, and then just take it step-by-step. Though technical, it is totally doable and definitely worth the extra effort.

Sponge Cake

2.50 oz Cake Mix

1 tsp baking powder

½ tsp salt

3 eggs, separated

3.50 oz sugar, divided

1 tsp vanilla extract

1 tsp lemon extract

1.50 oz butter, melted

¼ tsp cream of tartar

*Filling ingredients found on next page.

Preheat oven to 350°F. Coat 9-inch round springform pan with cooking spray and line with parchment.

This recipe calls for two stand mixers or one stand mixer and one hand mixer, both with whisk attachments. It is very important to *mise en place* this recipe to ensure accurate timing on all steps.

Cake

1. In small bowl, whisk together Cake Mix, baking powder, and salt. Set aside.

2. In bowl of stand mixer fitted with whisk attachment, whisk yolks on medium-high speed for approximately 2 minutes. See step #6 to ensure egg whites are whisking simultaneously.

3. After 2 minutes, gradually add 2.50 ounces of sugar to yolks. Whisk on medium for another two minutes until mixture is thick and pale yellow.

4. Whisk in extracts and melted butter until just combined.

5. Fold dry ingredients into yolk mixture by hand with spatula until just combined. Do not over mix.

6. While yolks are whisking (see step #2), in separate mixing bowl also fitted with whisk attachment, whisk egg whites and cream of tartar on high until frothy. You can also use a hand mixer here with balloon whisk attachment.

7. Once whites are frothy, slowly add remaining sugar and whisk on medium speed until stiff peaks form.

8. Fold half of whites into yolk batter. Be sure to fold in long, even strokes getting bottom of bowl as well as sides. Once mostly incorporated, fold remaining whites into batter until just combined.

9. Pour batter into prepared springform pan and bake for 16 minutes until light golden brown and center of cake springs back when touched. Allow sponge cake to cool while preparing filling.

Filling

32 oz cream cheese, softened and divided

12.50 oz sugar, divided

1.25 oz tapioca starch

1 Tbsp vanilla extract

1 egg

2 egg yolks

4 oz heavy cream

2.50 oz sour cream

Filling + Assembly

1. In stand mixer fitted with paddle attachment, beat 8 ounces of cream cheese, 2.50 ounces of sugar, and tapioca starch on low speed until creamy.

2. Slowly add remaining 24 ounces of cream cheese while continuously beating mixture on medium-low. I like to break cream cheese into small chunks with my hands and add it that way. You can also cut room temperature cream cheese into ½-inch cubes. Either way, be sure to scrape down bottom and sides of bowl often with spatula to make sure all cream cheese is incorporated, ultimately making batter extra smooth.

3. Slowly stream in remaining sugar and vanilla extract, adjust mixer speed to medium and beat until incorporated. Scrape sides and bottom of bowl again before moving on.

4. Beat in egg and egg yolks one at a time on medium, mixing well after each addition.

5. Adjust mixer speed to low and beat in heavy cream and sour cream until just mixed. Scrape sides of bowl with spatula one last time to make sure all ingredients are fully incorporated.

6. Using spatula, pour cream cheese filling on top of baked sponge cake.

7. Place springform pan onto large, square sheet of foil. Fold foil up edges of pan to ensure no water can get in. Then place springform pan into large roasting pan (a 12-inch cake pan works well here too if you have one available – rimmed sheet pans do not work). Fill roasting pan with water (does not need to be hot) until it is 1-inch up sides of springform pan.

8. Carefully place in preheated oven and bake until center barely jiggles. This takes approximately 1 hour and 30 minutes. Rotate pan halfway through baking if you notice uneven browning on top of cheesecake. Be sure to also check water levels halfway though. If all water has evaporated, add more to pan.

9. Once cheesecake is done, immediately remove from roasting pan and remove foil from springform pan*. Cool on wire rack until it reaches room temperature; this takes a few hours. When room temperature, cover and refrigerate overnight to set.

10. The next day, remove cheesecake from springform pan and cut into desired quantity of slices. Top with fresh berries, whipped cream, or even a batch of homemade lemon curd (pg. #46), you really can't go wrong!

*Foil will still be hot to touch here so be careful not to burn yourself. I suggest wearing oven mitts to remove foil.

UNTRADITIONAL TARA-MISU

Yield: 8 ridiculously delicious slices

To be honest, I never had tiramisu before I wrote this recipe. In fact, it never even crossed my mind – neither as a product to sell at the bakery nor as a treat to make at home. It all came about, as many of RylieCakes products did, from a Celiac customer who was craving tiramisu. She hadn't eaten it in years and claimed it was all she wanted for her birthday. How could I say no?

I got out my arsenal of cookbooks and got to work researching tiramisu. What was it supposed to taste like? What was its texture like? What were the traditional ingredients? And that's where I ran into a problem.

We were pressed for time at the bakery as the customer wanted to pick up her tiramisu in just 48 hours, which left me no time to recipe test and perfect gluten free lady fingers and then incorporate them into a cake I've never made before! So, I decided to get creative and use my tried and true separated sponge cake recipe to create cake layers rather than use the traditional ladyfingers.

My first ever and slightly Untraditional Tara-misu turned out marvelously! Our customer was thrilled – she loved it so much she ordered several more throughout the years – and the recipe went on to be a RylieCakes Original, nearly always stocked in the bakery case.

Sponge Cake

5 oz Cake Mix

2 tsp baking powder

1 tsp salt

6 eggs, separated

7 oz sugar, divided

2 tsp vanilla extract

2 tsp lemon extract

3 oz butter, melted

½ tsp cream of tartar

Soaking Syrup

6 oz strongly brewed coffee

1.50 oz hazelnut liqueur

2 Tbsp powdered sugar

1 tsp cinnamon

Filling

12 oz mascarpone

3.50 oz powdered sugar, sifted

1 Tbsp vanilla extract

1 Tbsp hazelnut liqueur

QS orange zest to flavor

12 oz heavy cream

Garnish

¼ cup cocoa powder

QS espresso beans

53

Preheat oven to 325°F. Coat two 7-inch square cake rings with cooking spray and place on sheet pan lined with parchment*. Chill mixing bowl with whisk attachment in your refrigerator or freezer until you are ready to make filling.

This recipe calls for two stand mixers or one stand mixer and one handheld mixer, both with whisk attachments. It is very important to *mise en place* this recipe to ensure accurate timing on all steps.

Cake

1. In small bowl, whisk together Cake Mix, baking powder, and salt. Set aside.

2. In bowl of stand mixer fitted with whisk attachment, whisk yolks on medium-high speed for approximately 2 minutes. See step #6 to ensure egg whites are whisking simultaneously.

3. After 2 minutes, gradually add 5 ounces of sugar to yolks. Whisk on medium speed for another 2 minutes until mixture is thick and pale yellow.

4. Whisk in extracts and melted butter until just combined.

5. Fold dry ingredients into yolk mixture by hand with spatula until just combined. Do not over mix.

6. While yolks are whisking (see step #2), in separate mixing bowl also fitted with whisk attachment, whisk egg whites and cream of tartar on high until frothy. You can also use a hand mixer here with balloon whisk attachment.

7. Once whites are frothy, slowly add remaining sugar and whisk on medium until stiff peaks form.

8. Fold half of whites into yolk batter. Be sure to fold in long, even strokes getting bottom of bowl as well as sides. Once mostly incorporated, fold remaining whites into batter until just combined.

9. Divide batter evenly into prepared cake squares. Bake for 16 minutes until light golden brown and center of cake springs back when touched. Allow sponge cake to cool while preparing soaking syrup and filling.

Soaking Syrup

1. Whisk together all syrup ingredients in 8 ounce liquid measuring cup and set aside.

Filling

1. In stand mixer fitted with chilled bowl and chilled whisk attachment, whip mascarpone and powdered sugar on medium until doubled in size.

2. Add vanilla extract, hazelnut liqueur, and orange zest into heavy cream. Slowly pour heavy cream mixture into mascarpone while continuing to whip on medium. Whip until stiff peaks form – be patient, it takes a few minutes but will come together**.

Assembly

1. Remove cake layers from cake squares if you haven't already. Place one layer on square cake board, cutting board, or flat serving plate.

2. Soak top of plated cake square very generously with soaking syrup using a pastry brush; use approximately one third of syrup.

3. Scoop half of mascarpone filling onto cake and spread evenly over top with small offset spatula. Be sure to get filling into each corner. Run backside of offset spatula along all four edges so that filling and cake line up evenly on all sides.

4. Soak one side of second cake layer using half of remaining soaking syrup and then carefully place it soaked side down on top of mascarpone filling. Using remaining syrup, soak top of second cake layer.

5. Spread remaining filling evenly over top of second layer. Again, be sure to frost all corners and run backside of offset spatula along all edges so that filling and cake line up evenly. It is okay to smear some of the frosting along the sides. In fact, I think it gives this cake a great rustic look.

6. Sift cocoa powder over top of cake until it is fully covered and then decorate with espresso beans. Refrigerate cake for at least 4 hours before serving; overnight is best.

*If you do not have 7-inch square cake rings, you can use two 8-inch square cake pans. Reduce baking time by 2 minutes to accommodate the thinner layers. Cake will not end up as high as pictured but will be just as tasty.

**If struggling with mascarpone filling, you can use cream cheese in place of mascarpone. It is more stable than mascarpone, making it easier to work with and whip.

cookies

HAMILTON HALF-MOON COOKIES

Yield: 14 divine cookies

I started out my college career at Hamilton – a quaint, private, liberal arts school in Upstate New York. It was a charming school set in a picturesque countryside with rolling hills, happy cows, and old-fashioned cider mills. Hamilton was nestled in Clinton; a tiny town consisting of a few mom and pop shops, some good restaurants, perfectly small bakeries and cafes, and of course, a local bar.

Whenever I had doctor's appointments that didn't go well (and there were many in those years), my girlfriend Francesca would always take me out for tea and sweet treats afterward in town. It was something I always looked forward to and it was on one of these trips that I discovered half-moon cookies. It was love at first bite.

I'm not sure why I never made these at the bakery, but when writing this book I thought it would be fun to add a few new recipes for those RylieCakes fans that have been around since day one – give them something new to chew on. And these Hamilton Half-Moon Cookies were perfect for the job. They are one of my favorite cookies and I have no doubt that they'll be one of your favorites too!

Cookies

9.50 oz Cake Mix

2 oz cocoa powder

1 tsp baking powder

¼ tsp salt

4 oz butter

8 oz sugar

1 egg

2.50 oz sour cream

1 tsp vanilla extract

5.50 oz buttermilk

Frosting

8 oz cream cheese, softened

4 oz butter, softened

12 oz powdered sugar, sifted

½ tsp almond extract

½ tsp vanilla extract

3 Tbsp cocoa powder

Preheat oven to 350°F. Line two half-sheet pans with silicone baking mats.

Cookies

1. Sift Cake Mix, cocoa powder, baking powder, and salt into medium bowl. Whisk to combine.

2. In stand mixer fitted with paddle attachment, cream butter and sugar until light and fluffy, approximately doubled in size.

3. Beat in egg on medium-low speed until well incorporated.

4. Add sour cream and vanilla extract. Beat to combine.

5. Adjust mixer to low, add buttermilk to batter and beat until just incorporated. Scrape bottom and sides of bowl.

6. Add dry ingredients and beat until smooth. Chill dough for 1 hour.

7. Portion dough into 14 uniform size cookies and bake 5 per pan; a blue scoop works perfect here.

8. Bake cookies for 14 minutes, rotating pan halfway through. Allow cookies to cool on pan for 10 minutes before transferring to wire rack to cool completely.

Frosting + Assembly

1. In bowl of stand mixer fitted with paddle attachment, beat cream cheese and butter together until completely smooth.

2. Add sifted powdered sugar and beat on medium speed until light, fluffy frosting consistency is reached. Add extracts and beat to combine.

3. Scoop half of the frosting into a small bowl, set aside. To original bowl of frosting, add cocoa powder and beat to combine. Use less cocoa for lighter frosting and more for a richer chocolate flavor and darker color.

4. Once cookies are cool, flip cookies over so that bottoms (flat sides) are facing up. Using small offset spatula, spread chocolate frosting over half of each cookie. Then cover the remaining half of each cookie with vanilla frosting.

SERIOUSLY ADDICTING SEA SALT BUTTERSCOTCH COOKIES

Yield: 18 out-of-this-world cookies

I always knew I was addicted to sweet treats; for as long as I can remember I've loved nearly everything that had to do with sugar. On any given day, you will find me munching away on sweets between the hours of 5 AM and 9 AM. I love my desserts for breakfast with many, many mugs of black coffee. At one point in time, I started getting hooked on cookies at night too.

It all started when I decided to bring home just one sea salt butterscotch cookie; it simply sounded so fricken' good. I ended up eating half the cookie and then, reluctantly, I decided to save the other half until morning. Out of pure laziness, I set the remaining half on my nightstand rather than bring it back down to the kitchen.

The next morning my alarm began singing and when I leaned over to turn it off, my fingers brushed against the cookie and I thought, "Why not?!" So I ate it as I started getting ready for the day. It was delightful – sweet and salty perfection.

I loved this new routine of mine so much, it carried on for another two weeks – half a sea salt butterscotch cookie at night, the remaining half at 4:30 AM the next morning. It was glorious! After two weeks, I realized I might have an addiction and much to my dismay, gave up my newest, most favorite habit immediately. Moral of the story: these cookies are seriously addicting – watch yourself!

---

8 oz butter, divided

Preheat oven to 325°F. Line half-sheet pans with silicon baking mats.

7.50 oz Cake Mix

1. Cut 6 ounces butter into grape-sized cubes. Place cubes in small saucepan over medium heat. Let butter melt and begin to bubble. To ensure butter is cooking evenly, rotate pan or tilt slightly to swirl butter around – do not stir. After a few minutes, bubbles will begin to fade and butter will change color. Watch closely at this point as it browns quickly from here. Butter is browned when it is dark golden in color and smells nutty.

7 oz Roux Mix

1¼ tsp baking soda

½ tsp salt

2. Once browned, immediately remove from heat and pour into bowl of stand mixer. Place bowl in refrigerator for a few hours until butter has solidified to match texture of room temperature butter.

10.50 oz brown sugar

3. While butter is chilling, whisk together Cake Mix, Roux Mix, baking soda, and salt in medium bowl. Set aside.

2 oz sugar

4. When brown butter is ready, add remaining 2 ounces butter and beat with paddle attachment on medium-high speed until completely smooth.

1 egg

5. Add both sugars and cream until light and fluffy, approximately doubled in size.

2 egg yolks

6. Add egg and egg yolks one at a time on low, beating shortly after each addition. Add vanilla bean paste and sour cream with last egg.

1 Tbsp vanilla bean paste

7. Add dry ingredients and beat until combined. Using spatula, scrape bottom and sides of bowl to ensure dough is thoroughly combined.

1 Tbsp sour cream

8. Add butterscotch chips and chocolate chips and mix until just combined. Chill dough for 1 hour.

7 oz butterscotch chips

9. Portion dough into 18 uniform size cookies and bake 5 per pan; a blue scoop works perfect here. Slightly flatten cookies with palm of hand.

7 oz chocolate chips

10. Bake for 16 minutes, rotating pan halfway through. As soon as you remove cookies from oven, sprinkle lavishly with sea salt flakes. Allow cookies to cool on pan for 10 minutes before transferring to wire rack to cool completely.

QS sea salt flakes

MOM'S DARK CHOCOLATE GINGER COOKIES

Yield: 17 marvelous cookies

During the recipe testing phase of starting the bakery, my Mom swooped into my test kitchen (a.k.a. her kitchen) and asked, "Do you have a cookie with ginger and dark chocolate?" I knew my mom well enough to know this wasn't a question but more of a statement: 110% suggesting that if I don't, I should, I must.

All night I was brainstorming. I envisioned these "spiced" cookies with layers of decadent dark chocolate and bursts of ginger, all tied together by something sweet… something sweet… by morning, it hit me: MOLASSES!

Rolling with it, I wrote up a recipe revolving around ginger, dark chocolate, and molasses and threw together a batch. My mom liked them but she didn't love them. I went back to the drawing board and tweaked a few more things: amped up my spice game, added more ginger, shimmied in some sea salt, and switched over to dark chocolate chunks rather than morsels. Holy Cow. This second batch of cookies were money! If my Mom didn't like them, I didn't care; they were that good.

Luckily, my Mom loved them and for years to come, I always got to tell customers that these cookies were inspired by, and made for, my one and only Mom.

8.50 oz Roux Mix

4 oz Cake Mix

2 Tbsp cocoa powder

1½ tsp baking soda

2 tsp ground ginger

1½ tsp cinnamon

1 tsp allspice

½ tsp sea salt

¼ tsp nutmeg

6 oz butter, softened

5.25 oz brown sugar

1 oz fresh ginger, peeled and finely chopped

5 oz molasses

11 oz dark chocolate chunks

3 oz sugar (for rolling)

Preheat oven to 325°F. Line half-sheet pans with parchment.

1. Sift Roux Mix, Cake Mix, cocoa powder, baking soda, ground ginger, cinnamon, allspice, sea salt, and nutmeg into medium bowl and whisk to combine. Set aside.

2. In stand mixer fitted with paddle attachment, cream butter and brown sugar until light and fluffy, approximately doubled in size.

3. Slowly add dry ingredients to butter mixture, beating on low speed until well combined.

4. Add fresh ginger and molasses. Beat until just combined. Using spatula, scrape bottom and sides of bowl to ensure dough is thoroughly combined.

5. Mix in chocolate chunks until just combined. Chill dough for 1 hour.

6. Portion dough into 17 uniform size cookies; a blue scoop works perfect here. Roll each cookie in sugar and slightly flatten with palm of hand. If dough gets too sticky while scooping and rolling, simply refrigerate again until firm, then finish process. Refrigerate cookies for 20 minutes before baking.

7. Transfer sugared cookies to prepared pans – 8 cookies per pan. Bake for 14 minutes, rotating pan halfway through.

8. Allow cookies to cool on pan for 10 minutes before transferring to wire rack to cool completely. These cookies only get better with time so no need to rush at scarfing them down!

BRENDA'S PEANUT BUTTER COOKIES

Yield: 14 fantastic cookies

I remember right after the grand opening of RylieCakes, my lifetime best friend Brenda – seriously, we've known each other since we were 5! – texted me to say that she just can't get enough of my peanut butter cookies. For years following, when she'd come to the bakery or I'd go to visit her, all she ever wanted was a peanut butter cookie. Of all the homemade, small batch pastries to choose from, that's all she ever asked for.

I've always believed that the best things in life are the little things. Sharing these cookies with Brenda as we talked about our lives and laughed for hours – knowing the second round of cookies would only bring about even more joy and laughter – has been one of the best little things for me in my life.

I swear, these super easy, extra creamy, devilishly delicious cookies will bring more happiness into your life than you ever imagined a cookie could!

16.80 oz creamy peanut butter

11.25 oz sugar

3.50 oz brown sugar

2 eggs

2 tsp baking soda

½ tsp salt

2 tsp vanilla extract

1.50 oz sugar (for rolling)

Preheat oven to 350°F. Line half-sheet pans with parchment.

1. In stand mixer fitted with paddle attachment, beat together peanut butter and sugars until smooth.

2. Beat in eggs one at a time on medium speed, beating 30 seconds after each addition.

3. Add baking soda, salt, and vanilla extract and beat until just combined.

4. Portion dough into 14 uniform size cookies; a blue scoop works perfect here. Using fork dipped in sugar, make crisscross pattern on cookies. Chill cookies for 1 hour before baking; bake 6 cookies per pan.

5. Bake for 16 minutes, rotating pan halfway through. Bake for a few extra minutes if you prefer crunchier cookies.

6. Allow cookies to cool on pan for 10 minutes before transferring to wire rack to cool completely. Don't be surprised when these cookies don't even last a day in your house!

Note: To add a bit more sweetness to these already delicious cookies, roll scooped cookies in sugar and flatten slightly before baking (skip fork crisscross). Immediately after removing from oven, dunk a Hershey® Kiss right in the center of each cookie.

UNDERRATED WHITE CHOCOLATE MACADAMIA NUT COOKIES

Yield: 20 impressive cookies

When I was a sophomore in high school, I was pretty much on top of the world as far as any 15-year-old-girl is concerned. I was class President, my boyfriend and I were crowned homecoming Prince and Princess, I had my driver's permit, and every weekend was spent at sleepovers with all my girlfriends. Life was good.

It was mid-October that year when my entire life was turned upside down. My dad had been in a boogie boarding accident and was temporarily paralyzed from the neck down. After three agonizing weeks of waiting for him to come home, he finally walked through the garage door late one night with my mom and uncle. For the next 8 months my dad recovered from home and we got the true pleasure of getting to spend more time with him. My dad's a goofy guy and no matter the situation, he can always find a way to make you laugh.

I remember at one point during his recovery my girlfriend Sally brought over some white chocolate macadamia nut cookies for him. That's actually the first time I remember eating white chocolate macadamia nut cookies and WOW, did they impress! After my first bite, all of my prior judgments were gone. These were some of the best cookies I had ever had. My dad full heartedly agreed with me and carried the cookies with him – on his head – everywhere he went so he didn't have to share!

I don't know what was so funny about watching my dad walk around slow as molasses in a neck brace with a plate of cookies on his head but to this day it still makes me laugh out loud. I hope these Underrated White Chocolate Macadamia Nut Cookies invade your home with merriment and laughter just as Sally's cookies did in ours so many years ago.

12.60 oz Roux Mix

3.75 oz Cake Mix

1 tsp baking soda

½ tsp salt

8 oz butter, softened

7 oz brown sugar

5.60 oz sugar

2 large eggs

1 egg yolk

2 tsp vanilla extract

1 tsp almond extract

10 oz white chocolate chips

6 oz macadamia nuts, roughly chopped

Preheat oven to 325°F. Line half-sheet pans with silicon baking mats.

1. Whisk together Roux Mix, Cake Mix, baking soda, and salt in medium bowl. Set aside.

2. In stand mixer fitted with paddle attachment, cream butter and both sugars until light and fluffy, approximately doubled in size.

3. Add eggs and egg yolk one at a time on medium speed, beating 30 seconds after each addition. Add both extracts with last egg.

4. Adjusting mixer to low, beat in dry ingredients until combined. Using spatula, scrape bottom and sides of bowl to ensure dough is thoroughly combined.

5. Add white chocolate chips and macadamia nuts, mix until just combined. Chill dough for 1 hour.

6. Portion dough into 20 uniform size cookies and bake 6 per pan; a blue scoop works perfect here. Slightly flatten cookies with palm of hand.

7. Bake for 18 minutes, rotating pan halfway through. Allow cookies to cool on pan for 10 minutes before transferring to wire rack to let cool completely.

OPA'S OATMEAL CRAISIN COOKIES

Yield: 22 delicious cookies

Just like my friend Brenda – who only ever wanted a peanut butter cookie (pg. #64) – Opa only ever wanted an oatmeal craisin cookie. Of all the pies, tarts and tortes, cakes and cupcakes, cookies, mousses, brownies and bars, Opa ALWAYS, without fail, chose an oatmeal craisin cookie.

You can't blame him. They have this crisp, lace-like outer edge with soft, pillowy centers simply bursting with flavor! Each bite greets your taste buds with morsels of melted, velvety chocolate, bits of sweet and tangy dried cranberries, and punches of that unique, naturally nectarous flavor of apricot. It's surely a mouthful, but it's the most insanely delicious mouthful you'll ever have!

And if you want to be just like Opa, slurp down a slightly sweetened vanilla latte while you're at it.

---

5 oz Cake Mix

1.40 oz Roux Mix

10.20 oz rolled oats

½ tsp baking soda

1 tsp salt

8 oz butter, softened

7 oz brown sugar

3.75 oz sugar

2 eggs

2 tsp vanilla extract

3 oz dried cranberries

3.50 oz dried apricots, finely chopped

6.50 oz semi-sweet chocolate chips

Preheat oven to 325°F. Line half-sheet pans with silicon baking mats.

1. Whisk together Cake Mix, Roux Mix, rolled oats, baking soda, and salt in medium bowl. Set aside.

2. In stand mixer fitted with paddle attachment, cream butter and both sugars until light and fluffy, approximately doubled in size.

3. Add eggs one at a time on medium speed, beating 30 seconds after each addition. Add vanilla extract with last egg.

4. Adjust mixer to low and beat in dry ingredients until just combined. Using spatula, scrape bottom and sides of bowl to ensure dough is thoroughly combined.

5. Add dried cranberries, chopped apricots, and chocolate chips and beat until incorporated. Chill dough for 1 hour.

6. Portion dough into 22 uniform size cookies and bake 5 per pan; a blue scoop works perfect here. Slightly flatten cookies with palm of hand.

7. Bake for 16 minutes, rotating pan halfway through.

8. Allow cookies to cool on sheet pan for 10 minutes before transferring to wire rack to cool completely. Devour as you please.

(TOO) SHAREABLE SHORTBREAD

Yield: 24 scrumptious cookies

Growing up, shortbread was never a cookie that was really on my radar. I don't have fond memories of my Oma, Nanny, or Mother making shortbread and I don't remember them being a staple of any family gathering. It is a funny thing though – you see shortbread gets the "short" part of its name because when you add fat (butter) to dough it weakens the bond between the water and flour. And what is that bond you may ask? Gluten.

When water and flour are combined, long strands of the protein gluten are formed. The more butter that is then added to the dough, the more its gluten strands are shortened. It is this process that causes shortbread to have such a rich, crumbly texture. You'd think it would be a no-brainer for a gluten free pastry chef to make shortbread given that it requires essentially no gluten network, but no, I didn't even think of it.

One day, I did eventually see the light, and we started making shortbread at the bakery like it was nobody's business. The more we made it, the more I couldn't stop eating it! Where had this simple, buttery cookie been my whole life? I also couldn't help but share; I didn't want any other soul out there to live as long as I did without this (Too) Shareable Shortbread. As the title implies, these mighty little cookies may be a little *too* shareable so make sure you stash some away from the get go – heaven forbid you ever run out!

---

7 oz butter, softened

3.75 oz sugar

1 tsp salt

1 tsp vanilla bean paste

11 oz Shortbread Mix

QS sparkling sugar

Preheat oven to 300°F. Line 8-inch square cake pan and two half-sheet pans with parchment.

1. In stand mixer fitted with paddle attachment, cream butter and sugar until light and fluffy, approximately doubled in size.

2. Add salt and vanilla bean paste, mix until just incorporated.

3. Adjust mixer to low, add Shortbread Mix and beat until just combined.

4. Place dough into center of prepared 8-inch square cake pan. Using cool hands, press dough evenly into shape of square. Refrigerate dough for 30 minutes.

5. Remove dough from pan by pulling up on parchment edges. Leaving dough on parchment, coat rolling pin with cooking spray and roll dough into 9-inch square. Dough should be evenly distributed and level on top. Use bench scraper to push up against sides of dough to form straight edges. If dough has softened, place back in refrigerator. Once firm again, finish shaping.

6. Using sharp knife, score cold dough. Mark dough 3 times on one edge to create four even sections. Then mark dough 5 times on perpendicular edge to create six even sections, creating 24 (2.25-inch by 1.50-inch) cookies. Double check to make sure marks are correct and dough is firm before you cut all the way through.

7. Arrange cookies on prepared pans leaving at least 1-inch between cookies. Sprinkle with sparkling sugar. Refrigerate for 2 hours in order to firm up one last time.

8. Bake approximately 28 minutes, rotating pan halfway through. Cookies will puff slightly and turn pale golden-brown when done. Allow cookies to cool on pans for 10 minutes before transferring to wire rack to cool completely. Store in an airtight container at room temperature.

Note: If you don't want center of cookies to rise slightly while baking, simply prick each cookie with a fork right in the center before placing in oven.

SWEET, SWEET SNICKERDOODLES

Yield: 15 oh-so-sweet cookies

When RylieCakes was first started, my goal was simply to create all the basics and then add on products from there depending on customer demand. What I didn't expect was that my "basics" would be different from everyone else's. I should have known that would be the case – I mean, what's really "the norm" anyways?

One of the "basics" I failed to create at the time was snickerdoodle cookies and I swear snickerdoodle fans came out of the woodwork in full force to let me know the error of my ways! How dare I not sell snickerdoodles?

It really doesn't take much to convince me to create a new product. I love both the recipe writing and recipe testing process. I find it so fascinating to see what difference a ¼ tsp less salt or a ½ tsp more cream of tartar can do to one batch of cookies. Science, man! It never ceases to amaze me. Needless to say, I was easily convinced to get my snickerdoodle on.

I played around in the kitchen and almost overnight, these Sweet, Sweet Snickerdoodles became a staple at RylieCakes. They are sinfully soft, light-as-air, perfectly chewy, and lathered in cinnamon-sugar; everything you could ever want from a cookie and more! I can proudly say snickerdoodles are now near the top of my list when it comes to baking basics.

Dough

11.25 oz Cake Mix

2 oz coconut flour

1½ tsp cream of tartar

1 tsp baking soda

¼ tsp baking powder

¼ tsp salt

8 oz butter, softened

11.50 oz sugar

2 eggs

1 egg yolk

1 Tbsp vanilla extract

For Rolling

2 oz sugar

1 Tbsp cinnamon

Preheat oven to 325°F. Line half-sheet pans with parchment.

1. Whisk together Cake Mix, coconut flour, cream of tartar, baking soda, baking powder, and salt in medium bowl. Set aside.

2. In stand mixer fitted with paddle attachment, cream butter and sugar until light and fluffy, approximately doubled in size.

3. Add eggs and egg yolk one at a time, beating well after each addition. Add vanilla extract with last egg.

4. Gradually add dry ingredients, beating on medium speed until thoroughly combined. Chill dough for 1 hour.

5. Combine sugar and cinnamon in small bowl for rolling.

6. Portion dough into 15 uniform size cookies; a blue scoop works perfect here. Roll cookies in cinnamon-sugar before placing onto prepared pans, 5 cookies per pan. Slightly flatten cookies with palm of hand.

7. Bake for 16 minutes, rotating pan halfway through.

8. Allow cookies to cool on pan for 10 minutes before transferring to wire rack to cool completely. Enjoy every bite, savor every last morsel!

CLASSIC CHOCOLATE CHIP COOKIES

Yield: 22 melt-in-your-mouth cookies

After I graduated from culinary school, I was set to move back home to Seattle and start up my own bakery. Though my mind was filled with wild dreams and ginormous goals, I had no place to live. So, like most twenty-somethings, I moved into my parent's basement. It was a mutually beneficial arrangement: my parents are a hoot and easy to be around and I was recipe testing for the bakery day in and day out, creating a sweetness in the air and countless fresh-from-the-oven treats.

One weekend, my friend had come over to catch up. She, my parents, and I were all chitchatting away in the kitchen over drinks while I was working up a batch of chocolate chip cookies. I was super excited to make these cookies because not only had I perfected my recipe, but my Dad loves, loves, loves chocolate chip cookies.

I was giddy with anticipation as I pulled the sheet pan out of the oven. The cookies looked so darn scrumptious! Light golden brown, perhaps a little gooey in places, the chocolate chips still melty... After five agonizing minutes of whiffing in their marvelous, rich, sweet fragrance, we finally decided to dive in. I could tell by the look on my dad's face that he was in love; with each bite his smile got wider and his "mmmms" louder. With another bite his expression changed rapidly and I frantically asked what was wrong.

He then used two fingers to delicately pull a small piece of what looked like paper out of his mouth. My dad had a good chuckle before recommending that I take off the entire butter wrapper before making cookies at the bakery. HA! So, word to the wise, fully unwrap your butter before creaming it. If you do that, I promise you these Classic Chocolate Chip Cookies won't let you down. You'll be thinking about making your next batch before you even finish your first!

11.50 oz Roux Mix

4 oz Cake Mix

1 tsp baking soda

¾ tsp salt

8 oz butter, softened

8.75 oz brown sugar

5.50 oz sugar

2 eggs

1 egg yolk

1½ Tbsp vanilla bean paste

17.50 oz chocolate chips (milk, semi-sweet, or dark)

Preheat oven to 325°F. Line half-sheet pans with silicon baking mats.

1. Whisk together Roux Mix, Cake Mix, baking soda, and salt in medium bowl. Set aside.

2. In stand mixer fitted with paddle attachment, cream together butter and sugars until light and fluffy, approximately doubled in size.

3. Add eggs and egg yolk one at a time on medium speed, beating 30 seconds after each addition. Add vanilla bean paste with last egg.

4. Adjust mixer to low, beat in dry ingredients until combined. Using spatula, scrape bottom and sides of bowl to ensure dough is thoroughly combined.

5. Add chocolate chips and mix until just combined. Chill dough for 1 hour.

6. Portion dough into 22 uniform size cookies and bake 8 per pan; a blue scoop works perfect here. Slightly flatten cookies with palm of hand.

7. Bake for 16 minutes, rotating pan halfway through.

8. Allow cookies to cool on pan for 10 minutes before transferring to wire rack to cool completely. Or if you can't resist that sweet, sweet smell any longer, just dig in!

GIGANTIC GINGER SNAPS

Yield: 14 cozy cookies

It was a cold, rainy, winter night in Seattle. The house had a chill but was warmed by the glow of the fire, and calmed by candlelight. Ben's buddy Jake had come into town for work and was staying with us over the weekend. It was always fun when Jake came to town; the three of us were incredible at kicking back and sipping on a drink or two while shooting the breeze for hours – this time bundled up in our favorite sweat pants and cozy sweatshirts. As we talked, played video games, and talked some more, I got the craving for something sweet so I moseyed into the kitchen to whip something up.

We really didn't have much in the house. I am almost ashamed to say it, but we didn't even have chocolate chips or an ample amount of peanut butter lying around! My mind was set on cookies, but the two classics were out. And then I found some crystallized ginger. I am no fan of eating candied ginger on its own, however, I could get onboard with it if smooshed into a mix of butter, sugar, and molasses. So I ended up making a batch of ginger snaps for a late night snack.

Boy, were we spoiled that night! The cookies were crisp and crunchy on the outside but still chewy in the center – the best of both worlds when it comes to ginger snaps if you ask me. We ate them for breakfast the following morning as well, only to find out they were even better than the night before! Now, not a winter goes by where I don't make these; I hope they become an absolute winter-must-have in your home, too.

---

7 oz Roux Mix

5 oz Cake Mix

1 tsp ground ginger

1 tsp cinnamon

½ tsp ground cloves

¼ tsp ground nutmeg

1 tsp baking soda

¼ tsp salt

6 oz butter, softened

7.50 oz sugar

2 oz molasses

1 egg

1 egg yolk

3½ oz crystallized ginger, finely chopped

QS demerara sugar

Preheat oven to 350°F. Line half-sheet pans with silicon baking mats.

1. Whisk together Roux Mix, Cake Mix, spices, baking soda, and salt in medium bowl. Set aside.

2. In stand mixer fitted with paddle attachment, cream butter and sugar until light and fluffy, approximately doubled in size.

3. Beat in molasses, egg, and egg yolk on medium-low speed until well combined.

4. Adjusting mixer to low, beat in dry ingredients until combined. Using spatula, scrape bottom and sides of bowl to ensure dough is thoroughly combined.

5. Add chopped ginger and beat until just combined. Chill dough for 1 hour.

6. Portion dough into 14 uniform size cookies; a blue scoop works perfect here. Roll each cookie in demerara sugar and slightly flatten with palm of hand. Refrigerate dough for 15 minutes before baking.

7. Transfer sugared cookies to prepared pans – 5 cookies per pan. Bake for 14 minutes, rotating pan halfway through.

8. Allow cookies to cool on pan for 10 minutes before transferring to wire rack to cool completely. These cookies only get better with time. Once they cool, store in an airtight container at room temperature and eat leisurely throughout the week.

MEGHAN'S TREMENDOUS TRIPLE CHOCOLATE BALSAMIC COOKIES

Yield: 30 brilliant cookies

When I lived in Arizona, I had few friends. Mostly because I was so busy juggling school, doctor appointments, and being exhausted that I chose to hang out with my dog most of the time. Nowadays, I'd like to think I have a lot of friends and yet, I still choose to hang out with my dog and cat most of the time…

Meghan was one of my few good friends in Arizona. She and I united on two fronts: we were both Economics Majors and we both loved to bake in our spare time. Our email and text correspondence would have been confusing to a third person as it often talked of the SEC, the Federal Reserve, over-leveraging, conflicts of interest and so on, followed immediately by "I'd use a heaping teaspoon of sea salt and agave if you have it." Meghan was actually the first person I called when I decided to open RylieCakes; I wanted her so badly to join me on the adventure. To this day, she is still one of the most magical chefs I know.

Meghan made the original recipe for these Tremendous Triple Chocolate Balsamic Cookies; they were egg free and astounding! I remember the first time I ate one and was absolutely blown away.

I have tweaked the recipe over the years to make it gluten free and threw in some curveballs along the way – like sour cream to accompany the tartness of the vinegar – all of which have made them equally delicious to Meghan's original melt-in-your-mouth masterpieces.

5.60 oz Roux Mix

2.50 oz Cake Mix

¼ tsp baking soda

¼ tsp salt

5.80 oz semi-sweet chocolate chips

4 oz butter, softened

3.50 oz brown sugar

3.75 oz sugar

2 eggs

1 Tbsp sour cream

½ tsp vanilla bean paste

1 Tbsp balsamic vinegar

5 oz white chocolate chips

2.50 oz milk chocolate chips

Preheat oven to 350°F. Line half-sheet pans with silicon baking mats.

1. Whisk together Roux Mix, Cake Mix, baking soda, and salt in medium bowl. Set aside.

2. Melt semi-sweet chocolate chips in microwave safe bowl until smooth. Microwave in 30 second increments and stir between each set so as to not burn chocolate. Set aside.

3. In bowl of stand mixer fitted with paddle attachment, cream together butter and sugars until light and fluffy, approximately doubled in size.

4. Add eggs one at a time, beating well after each addition.

5. Add sour cream, vanilla bean paste, and balsamic vinegar. Beat on low speed until just combined.

6. Slowly stream in melted chocolate and beat until just combined.

7. Add dry ingredients and beat until fully incorporated.

8. Add white and milk chocolate chips. Beat until just combined. Chill dough for 1 hour.

9. Portion dough into 30 uniform size cookies and bake 11 per pan; a black scoop works perfect here.

10. Bake for 12 minutes, rotating pan halfway through. Cookies will look puffy in center when done.

11. Allow cookies to cool on pan for 10 minutes before transferring to wire rack to cool completely. Give these cookies 24 hours for the flavors to meld before digging in.

THE BEST EVER VEGAN CHOCOLATE CHIP COOKIES

Yield: 18 magical cookies

Chocolate chip cookies are a classic – always have been, always will be. When I decided that RylieCakes needed some vegan treats added to its every day line-up, there was no better place to start than good ol' chocolate chip cookies.

What I didn't know then was that these, The Best Ever Vegan Chocolate Chip Cookies, would gain such a reputation that we'd start receiving phone calls as soon as we opened from customers wanting to buy everything we had in stock that day. They were truly magical and the smile they brought to customers' faces was unreal – seriously, you wouldn't believe people could smile that big!

After closing the bakery, I continued to receive weekly emails from customers about how sad they were to see us go, but one email stood out in particular. This customer wrote me over half a page describing how delicious our vegan chocolate chip cookies were and finished it up with how much he missed them. He commented on how he was instantly blown away the first time he tried them; saying he felt like he was eating a cookie filled with gluten again. He also said that they were the best gluten free, vegan chocolate chip cookie in all of Seattle and I'd have to agree.

Whether you're vegan or not, you definitely want to add these cookies to your baking queue immediately!

---

3 oz coconut oil, melted

3 oz canola oil

10 oz brown sugar

3 oz coconut cream

1½ tsp vanilla extract

14.25 oz Vegan Cookie Mix

10 oz vegan mini chocolate chips

Preheat oven to 325°F. Line half-sheet pans with silicon baking mats.

1. In stand mixer fitted with paddle attachment, beat together coconut oil, canola oil, and brown sugar on medium speed for 1 minute. Scrape bottom and sides of bowl with spatula.

2. Adjust mixer to medium-high, add coconut cream and vanilla extract and beat for 1 minute until thick and creamy.

3. Add Vegan Cookie Mix and beat on low until just combined.

4. Add vegan mini chocolate chips and beat until incorporated.

5. Chill dough in airtight container and refrigerate overnight. If you want them right away (I know the feeling!), refrigerate dough for at least 4 hours to set up.

6. Portion dough into 18 uniform size cookies and bake 5 per pan; a blue scoop works perfect here.

7. Bake 16 minutes, rotating pan halfway through. Edges should look crisp and golden brown while centers should still look a little ooey gooey when done.

8. Be sure to keep cookie dough refrigerated in between batches. Seriously, I'm not just suggesting!

9. Let cookies cool on pan for approximately 10 minutes before transferring to wire rack to cool completely. Or gobble them up warm before anyone else can get their hands on them – I won't tell anyone!

Note: This dough holds for weeks in the freezer and bakes great when frozen. Freeze pre-portioned dough and bake fresh when you have a craving.

UNBEATABLE BANANADOODLES

Yield: 16 heavenly cookies

When we first started making Unbeatable Bananadoodles at RylieCakes, our customers were thrilled! They loved the crisp, sugary, golden edges that surrounded the light, fluffy center slamming their taste buds with hints of cinnamon and bursts of banana. Each carefully crafted cookie was just right – not too much banana, not too much fluff, never too much sugar – each fit for the vegan gods.

What customers didn't know was that these cookies made even the most badass Pastry Chefs cry! You may be laughing out loud right now but I am so serious! Perfecting these cookies to what they are today took hours, weeks, and months of making minor adjustments, tweaking not only ingredients but also the process itself.

That being said, these Unbeatable Bananadoodles, though heavenly when done, can be a real pill if you don't follow each and every step. I know there is a lot of freezing overnight when you just want to eat the darn cookies, but I promise you, the wait is so worth it!

Dough

2 large bananas

4 oz canola oil

3 oz coconut cream

10 oz sugar

1 Tbsp molasses

1 Tbsp vanilla extract

12.50 oz Vegan Cookie Mix

For Rolling

2 oz sugar

1 Tbsp cinnamon

Day 1

1. Chop each banana into 10 pieces, place in airtight container and freeze overnight.

Day 2

1. Using stand mixer fitted with paddle attachment, beat oil, coconut cream, sugar, molasses, and vanilla extract on medium-high speed until light in color and creamy. This takes approximately 2 minutes.

2. Adjust mixer to medium and add frozen, pre-chopped banana pieces. Beat until the majority of banana pieces are broken down. A few small chunks are just fine!

3. Adjust mixer to low, add Vegan Cookie Mix and beat until just combined. Batter will be loose; do not let this scare you!

4. Place dough in an airtight container and refrigerate overnight.

Day 3

Preheat oven to 350°F. Line half-sheet pans with silicon baking mats.

1. Combine sugar and cinnamon for rolling in small bowl.

2. Portion dough into 16 uniform size cookies; a blue scoop works perfect here. Place cookies in freezer for 30 minutes to let dough set one more time.

3. Roll dough in cinnamon-sugar mixture and place on prepared pans, 5 cookies per pan.

4. Immediately after rolling, bake cookies for 18 minutes, rotating pan halfway through. Keep remaining dough in freezer until ready to bake. Cookies are done when outsides are crisp and golden brown and centers are slightly doughy.

5. Let cookies cool on pan for 15 minutes before transferring to wire rack to cool completely.

6. Bananadoodles are very delicate – handle with care. They also do not freeze well after being baked. If you would like to keep some for future use, I recommend freezing pre-scooped and pre-rolled dough.

Note: Making sure your dough is cold enough to work with is essential for this recipe. Do not skip any freezing or refrigerating steps!

HOMEMADE HONEY GRAHAM CRACKERS

Yield: 25 totally snackable cookies or 21 ounces cookie crumbs

Growing up, my brother and I had a babysitter in the neighborhood. It was a pretty sweet deal because we would go to her house everyday, but still be able to play with all of our friends in the neighborhood and go home if we needed to grab anything. Sue, our babysitter, was really incredible; she'd take us to parks, the library, other fun events around town, and she made the best BBQ chicken pizza ever!! However, she was also known to be the "Snack Police".

Sue would portion out all snacks and prepackage them. When it was snack time, we could choose one snack from Bin A or two from Bin B. Of those perfectly portioned treats were graham crackers, two sheets or eight crackers, however you'd like to look at it. And they were good but never, ever enough!

When I finally got around to making my own graham crackers, my only goal was to make them so completely irresistible that eating only two would never even be an option. And these Homemade Graham Crackers do just that! They are light, slightly sweet, totally crunchy, and smothered in cinnamon-sugar. You and your family are bound to fall in love and enjoy them for years to come!

Dough	Preheat oven to 325°F. Line half-sheet pans with parchment.
8.40 oz Roux Mix	1. Combine Roux Mix, Cake Mix, brown sugar, baking powder, baking soda, salt, and cinnamon in bowl of food processor and pulse to combine.
2.50 oz Cake Mix	
3.50 oz brown sugar	2. Add cubed, chilled butter to food processor and pulse until butter breaks down to size of peas.
½ tsp baking powder	3. Add honey, molasses, and vanilla extract and process until dough starts to take form of a ball, pulling away from edges. Mixture will still be crumbly.
½ tsp baking soda	4. Remove dough from food processor and flatten into shape of disk. Tightly wrap dough in plastic wrap and chill for 1 hour or overnight if possible.
¼ tsp salt	5. After chilling, remove dough from refrigerator and place on parchment. Liberally coat rolling pin with cooking spray and roll out dough to an 1/8-inch thickness.
¼ tsp cinnamon	
4 oz butter, cut into ½" cubes and chilled	6. Using round 3-inch fluted cookie cutter, cut out graham crackers. Transfer from rolling surface to prepared pans, leaving 1-inch between cookies. Reroll scraps of dough to finish cutting out cookies.
4 oz honey	7. Refrigerate cookie cutouts for 30 minutes before baking.
1 Tbsp molasses	8. After final chill, whisk together sugar and cinnamon in small bowl. Then sprinkle over cookies.
1 tsp vanilla extract	9. Bake for 20 minutes, rotating pan halfway through. For chewier cookies, bake a few minutes less.
Topping	10. Remove cookies from oven and let cool on pan for 10 minutes before transferring to wire rack to cool completely.
2 oz sugar	11. Store in airtight container at room temperature once completely cooled. Dip in chocolate, take camping, make s'mores, pack in school lunches, or just munch on like there is no tomorrow. Every way is the right way to eat these cookies!
1 Tbsp cinnamon	

CANDICE'S PB OATMEAL COOKIE SANDWICHES

Yield: 16 scrumptious sandwich cookies

Candice Bledsoe is an amazing woman. I have to toot her horn really quick because RylieCakes Bakery and this book would have never been possible without her! She did nearly all the photography for the bakery and was my layout designer for this very book. On top of her stunning work, which happened to make all my food look downright mouthwatering, she puts up with me! Candice so kindly works with my detail-oriented perfectionism and for that, I am incredibly grateful.

All that being said, Candice and I have two things very much in common: an obsession for color coding with fine-point pens and a love of pastries.

Years ago Candice asked if I could make homemade Nutter Butters® and without blinking an eye, I said yes! One, who doesn't love Nutter Butters®? And two, it's Candice, how could I say no?

Off I went and created my take on Nutter Butters®. I came up with these puffy, chewy oatmeal cookies sandwiched with heavenly peanut butter cream filling. They were sensational. However, over the years Candice was diagnosed with an egg allergy. So without telling her, I decided to rework the recipe to make these cookies egg free for this book. I didn't think it was humanly possible but the cookies turned out even better than before!

Dough

3.75 oz Cake Mix

1.50 oz Roux Mix

5 oz rolled oats

½ tsp baking powder

½ tsp baking soda

¼ tsp salt

8 oz butter, softened

4.20 oz creamy peanut butter

7.50 oz sugar

3.75 oz brown sugar

2.25 oz bananas, mashed

1½ tsp vanilla extract

Filling

8 oz butter, softened

8.40 oz creamy peanut butter

10.75 oz powdered sugar, sifted

Preheat oven to 325°F. Line half-sheet pans with parchment.

Dough

1. Whisk together Cake Mix, Roux Mix, rolled oats, baking powder, baking soda, and salt in medium bowl. Set aside.

2. In stand mixer fitted with paddle attachment, beat butter and peanut butter until completely smooth and no lumps exist.

3. Add sugars and beat on medium speed until mixture is light and fluffy, approximately doubled in size.

4. Adjust mixer to low, add mashed banana and vanilla extract. Beat until just combined.

5. Add dry ingredients and beat until well incorporated. Using spatula, scrape bottom and sides of bowl to ensure dough is thoroughly combined. Chill dough for 2 hours or overnight if possible.

6. Portion dough into 32 uniform size cookies and bake 12 per pan; a purple scoop works perfect here. Slightly flatten cookies with palm of hand.

7. Bake for 18 minutes, rotating pan halfway through. Allow cookies to cool on pan for 10 minutes before transferring to wire rack to cool completely. While cooling, make filling.

Filling + Assembly

1. Cream together butter and peanut butter until completely smooth. Add sifted powdered sugar slowly, beating until smooth. Filling should be light and creamy.

2. Using purple scoop (or tablespoon), scoop filling onto the bottom of one cookie and sandwich together with another. Continue process until all cookies have been sandwiched. You will have some extra filling, which is great to simply eat by the spoonful or use as filling in your favorite cake.

brownies & bars

NOT-YOUR-GRANDMA'S SUGAR COOKIE BARS

Yield: 16 dreamy bars

During the recipe testing phase of this book, I met up with one of my recipe testers to go over which recipes she'd be working on and answer any questions for her. Betty's only question was, "Are sugar cookies going to be in the cookbook? I don't see them here." This brought a huge, awkward smile to face. I had to break the news to her that my sugar cookie recipe was not in the book.

On my way home, I couldn't shake the thought of Betty's disappointment but I stood by my decision to not add sugar cookies to the book. Though making sugar cookies is relatively easy, decorating them is a fussy process and I wanted to keep this cookbook as unfussy as possible. And then it came to me, why not make sugar cookie bars!

This recipe took me a few trial runs to figure out but once I did, I was in cookie bar heaven. They were everything you'd want in a sugar cookie – chewy, buttery, soft, and topped with sweet frosting – but made so much easier. Not a soul will be disappointed when they've found out you made these Not-Your-Grandma's Sugar Cookie Bars.

Cake

16.25 oz Cake Mix

1.40 oz Roux Mix

1 tsp baking soda

½ tsp salt

¼ tsp baking powder

8 oz butter

14 oz sugar

2 eggs

1 egg yolk

1 tsp almond extract

½ tsp vanilla bean paste

Frosting

8 oz cream cheese, softened

4 oz butter, softened

12 oz powdered sugar, sifted

½ tsp almond extract

½ tsp vanilla extract

QS food coloring (optional)

Topping

QS rainbow sprinkles

Preheat oven to 350°F. Coat 9-by-13-inch cake pan with cooking spray and line with parchment.

Cake

1. Whisk together Cake Mix, Roux Mix, baking soda, salt, and baking powder in medium bowl. Set aside.

2. In stand mixer fitted with paddle attachment, cream butter and sugar until light and fluffy, approximately doubled in size.

3. On medium-low speed, add eggs and egg yolk one at a time, beating well after each addition. Add almond extract and vanilla bean paste with last egg.

4. Slowly add dry ingredients and beat on low until thoroughly incorporated.

5. Scoop dough into prepared pan and press down into an even layer using hands.

6. Bake bars for 40 minutes, covering with foil and rotating pan halfway through. Bars are done when toothpick inserted into center comes out clean. Let cool on wire rack while making frosting.

Frosting

1. In bowl of stand mixer fitted with paddle attachment, beat cream cheese and butter together until completely smooth and no lumps exist.

2. Add sifted powdered sugar and beat on medium speed until light, fluffy frosting consistency is reached.

3. Add extracts, beat to combine. If you desire, add food coloring here to create more vibrant frosting options.

4. When bars have cooled to room temperature, remove from pan and spread frosting evenly over bars with offset spatula. Top generously with rainbow sprinkles.

SUNFLOWER-AGAVE GRANOLA BARS

Yield: 12 totally snackable bars

Beginning to write this headnote brings a huge smile to my face and makes me chuckle just a little out loud. These Sunflower–Agave Granola Bars brought us so much joy and frustration at the bakery.

There was one time a customer pulled me aside to discuss the chocolate chunk ratio in the granola bars. There was another time when a customer was upset because the chocolate slightly melted into the bars, which is what you get in an un-air-conditioned kitchen in the middle of summer in Seattle. Also, there was the time when we forgot about the pot of sunflower butter, applesauce, agave, and coconut oil on the stove and it literally EXPLODED EVERYWHERE! We were cleaning that one up for weeks! And then there was the time we cut the bars into the completely wrong shape and size on multiple full batches but ran with it anyways because we decidedly liked that shape better.

Though wicked easy to make, we clearly found ways to go wrong from time to time. The good news is, you don't have to make our mistakes. You can just enjoy the process and snack away on the goodness that ensues. These bars are not too sweet, crunchy, chewy, chocolaty, and tart, which I'm pretty sure checks all the boxes for best granola bars ever!

6.75 oz cinnamon applesauce

6.75 oz sunflower butter

5 oz agave

4 oz coconut oil

6 oz rolled oats

4 oz brown rice crisps

3 oz dried cherries, roughly chopped

3 oz dried mango, roughly chopped

1.50 oz roasted pumpkin seeds

1.50 oz roasted sunflower seeds

3.25 oz dark chocolate chunks

Coat 9-by-13-inch cake pan with cooking spray and line with parchment.

1. In large saucepan over medium heat, stir together applesauce, sunflower butter, agave, and coconut oil with a spatula until well combined. Sunflower butter should be fully dissolved into mixture when done. Mixture will be runny.

2. Remove from heat and stir in rolled oats, brown rice crisps, dried cherries and mango, and pumpkin and sunflower seeds.

3. Pour mixture into prepared pan and using small offset spatula, spread and press firmly down into even layer.

4. Press chocolate chunks into granola bars. If they start to melt, wait a few more minutes. Or if you don't mind them melty, shove them in!

5. Let bars cool to room temperature. Then cover and refrigerate for 4 hours to set.

6. Cut bars to whatever size and shape you'd like. I cut mine into 12 rectangles creating the perfect snack to grab and go. These bars last up to one month in your refrigerator though I doubt they will make it that long!

SINFUL TRIPLE CHOCOLATE CARAMEL BROWNIES

Yield: 9 generous squares

Brownies are a classic and have been part of my repertoire for quite a while now. However, these brownies took a major upgrade when I started making my own flour blends. My Cake Mix turned these brownies from basic bake sale brownies to glorious, out-of-this-world, award-worthy brownies. And to take it even further, I decided to start topping these bad boys off with not only fudge frosting, but also my homemade salted caramel sauce. Game over – you cannot make brownies any better than this!

Caramel Topping

1 batch salted caramel sauce

Batter

5 oz butter

2 oz cocoa powder

2.50 oz Cake Mix

¼ tsp salt

¼ tsp baking powder

8 oz sugar

2 eggs

1 tsp vanilla extract

7 oz semi-sweet chocolate chips

Frosting

3 oz butter, softened

4.25 oz powdered sugar

1 oz cocoa powder

1 oz honey

1 tsp vanilla extract

Topping

QS sea salt flakes

Preheat oven to 375°F. Coat 8-inch square cake pan with cooking spray and line with parchment.

Caramel Topping

1. Make one batch of Out-Of-This-World Salted Caramel Sauce (pg. #38) and set aside.

Batter

1. In large saucepan, melt butter. Once melted, remove from heat and let cool for 10 minutes.

2. While butter is cooling, whisk together cocoa powder, Cake Mix, salt, and baking powder in medium bowl. Set aside.

3. Once butter has cooled slightly, whisk in sugar, eggs, and vanilla extract until thoroughly combined.

4. Fold in dry ingredients with spatula until combined.

5. Fold in chocolate chips.

6. Pour batter into prepared pan and bake for 28 minutes, rotating pan halfway through. Brownies are done when toothpick inserted into center comes out with few moist crumbs. For more cake-like brownies, bake a few minutes longer. Set pan on wire rack to cool.

Frosting + Assembly

1. While brownies are baking, in bowl of stand mixer fitted with paddle attachment, cream butter and powdered sugar until light and fluffy, approximately doubled in size.

2. Add cocoa powder, honey, and vanilla extract. Beat on medium-high speed until light, whipped frosting forms.

3. Remove brownies from pan and remove parchment. Then, with offset spatula, smear frosting evenly over brownies.

4. Cut brownies into 9 generous squares and then spoon homemade salted caramel sauce over each brownie; I always like to spoon on a little extra caramel so it ever so slightly drips down sides of brownies. Lastly, sprinkle with sea salt flakes.

BELOVED BUTTERSCOTCH BLONDIES

Yield: 16 sweet, sweet squares

Oh my goodness, Blondies, people! It is all about the Blondies! Just one bite of these will satisfy any sweet tooth and even make the least likely butterscotch opponents fall in love. So skit-skat-skoodle-doot and get to making these most beloved bars.

---

6 oz butter

4 oz pecans

6.30 oz Cake Mix

1 tsp baking powder

¼ tsp salt

7 oz brown sugar

1 egg

1 egg yolk

1 tsp vanilla bean paste

5 oz butterscotch chips

Preheat oven to 375°F. Coat 8-inch square cake pan with cooking spray and line with parchment.

1. Cut butter into grape-sized cubes. Place cubes in small saucepan over medium heat. Let butter melt and begin to bubble. To ensure butter is cooking evenly, rotate pan or tilt slightly to swirl butter around – do not stir. After a few minutes, bubbles will begin to fade and butter will change color. Watch closely at this point as it browns quickly from here. Butter is browned when it is dark golden in color and smells nutty.

2. Once browned, immediately remove from heat and pour into bowl of stand mixer. Refrigerate bowl for a few hours until butter has solidified to match texture of room temperature butter.

3. While butter is chilling, line rimmed baking sheet with parchment, place pecans in single layer on parchment. Bake in preheated oven for 5 to 7 minutes until golden brown and have a nutty fragrance. Remove from oven, cool completely, and then roughly chop. Turn oven down to 325°F.

4. While butter and pecans are cooling, whisk together Cake Mix, baking powder, and salt in medium bowl. Set aside.

5. When brown butter is ready, beat with paddle attachment on medium-high speed until completely smooth.

6. Add brown sugar and cream mixture until light and fluffy, approximately doubled in size.

7. Add egg and egg yolk one at a time on medium, beating shortly after each addition. Add vanilla bean paste with last egg.

8. Adjust mixer to low, beat in dry ingredients until just combined.

9. Add butterscotch chips and chopped pecans, beat until incorporated. Using spatula, scrape bottom and sides of bowl to make sure batter is thoroughly combined.

10. Pour batter into prepared pan and level with offset spatula.

11. Bake for 24 minutes, rotating pan halfway through.

12. Remove from oven and let cool on wire rack until pan is cool to touch. Once cool to touch, remove bars from pan and continue to let cool on wire rack. These bars cut best once they've cooled down to room temperature.

13. Cut into 16 squares, share the love, and enjoy the smiles you've put on everyone's face!

WOODI'S PEANUT BUTTER JELLY BARS

Yield: 9 mouth-watering squares

When it comes to food I strongly believe in a balanced diet, eating everything in moderation. Some days I eat salads and drink protein smoothies and others I eat cake and lots of it. My brother, on the other hand, believes that everything in life should be extraordinarily extreme, and his lifestyle, of course, fits the bill.

Woodi once was a body builder and personal trainer. When he entered into competitions, he flipped his entire life upside down. He would eat six set meals at the same time each day; each meal would be meticulously prepped, weighed out, and consist of the same five or so ingredients – no sauces, no seasonings. I'm literally gasping for air just writing this! On top of this, he worked out multiple times a day, sat in saunas to lose water weight, and didn't drink any alcohol. This would go on for months at a time; imagine, no wine for months at a time!

After all of the crazy of extreme dieting, working out, and flexing his guns in a slim-cut bikini bottom, Woodi would eat as if he's never eaten before. He would spend a week eating guacamole, chips, pizza, wings, burgers, donuts, bagels, pancakes, and you've guessed it, Peanut Butter Jelly Bars!

These bars are so sinfully good and proven to be worth waiting for. Lucky for you, you don't have to!

Crust

5.75 oz graham crackers

1.25 oz slivered almonds

4 oz butter

2 oz sugar

1.25 oz cocoa powder

1 tsp salt

4 oz shredded coconut

Filling

1 batch Just A Minute Jam

4 oz butter, softened

4.20 oz creamy peanut butter

5.50 oz powdered sugar, sifted

Topping

6 oz dark chocolate chips

1 tsp coconut oil

2 oz shredded coconut, toasted

Coat 8-inch square cake pan with cooking spray and line with parchment.

Crust

1. Make one batch of Homemade Honey Graham Crackers (pg. #84) or buy premade gluten free graham crackers from the store.

2. Place graham crackers and almonds in food processor, pulse until crumb consistency is reached. Set aside.

3. In small saucepan, whisk together butter, sugar, and cocoa powder on low-medium heat. Stir until smooth.

4. Remove from heat and fold in crumb mixture, salt, and coconut until combined.

5. Pour crust into prepared pan and press down into even layer using hands. Place in freezer to set.

Filling

6. Make one batch of Just A Minute Jam (pg. #40) and set aside.

7. In mixing bowl fitted with paddle attachment, cream together butter and peanut butter until completely smooth.

8. Add sifted powdered sugar slowly, beating until smooth. Filling should be light and fluffy.

9. Remove pan with crust from freezer and spread peanut butter filling evenly over crust using small offset spatula.

10. Measure out 6.50 ounces of raspberry jam and spread evenly over peanut butter filling using same offset spatula. Place back in freezer for 30 minutes to set. Remaining raspberry jam can be refrigerated in an airtight container for future use – who's up for a PB & J sandwich?!

Topping

11. When 30 minutes is nearly up, melt chocolate in microwave until smooth. Be sure to melt in short increments of time to avoid burning.

12. Once fully melted, add coconut oil to loosen.

13. Remove pan from freezer and quickly spread melted chocolate over jam using small offset spatula.

14. Sprinkle toasted coconut on top. Place back in freezer for 1 hour to set.

15. Cut into nine generous squares to serve. Keep a glass of milk and a bin of napkins handy – these bars are outrageously decadent and extremely messy!

Note: In place of graham crackers you can use any kind of RylieCakes' cookies. Simply bake cookies a few minutes longer than suggested in order to get them crisp enough to crumb.

KATRINA'S FUDGEY OAT BARS

Yield: 16 scrumptious bars

Back in the day, when I could eat anything my little heart desired, my cousin Katrina and I used to love to go to Starbucks®. The main reason for our visits actually wasn't for the drinks at all – I didn't even drink coffee yet – we went for the Oat Fudge Bars. I remember them being these absolutely phenomenal, sweet, fudgey brownies that were healthy because they were chock full of oats. That's how it works, right?

When it came time to open the bakery, I figured some version of Oat Fudge Bars were a must, but of course, with my own touch added to them. I doubled the fudge filling from what I remembered and added a little cinnamon for some spice. In no time, my recipe exceeded my memories!

I hope you also devour a few too many of these smashing bars while cozying up with a coffee, or chai, in hand.

Blondie Base

12 oz Cake Mix

¾ tsp baking soda

5 oz rolled oats

4.50 oz butter, softened

10 oz brown sugar

3 eggs

2 tsp vanilla extract

Fudge Filling

1.50 oz butter

14 oz sweetened condensed milk

4 oz heavy cream

18 oz semi-sweet chocolate chips

Topping

2.25 oz rolled oats

2 tsp cinnamon

½ tsp salt

2 oz butter, melted

Preheat oven to 350°F. Coat 9-by-13-inch cake pan with cooking spray and line with parchment.

Blondie Base

1. Whisk together Cake Mix, baking soda, and rolled oats in medium bowl. Set aside.

2. In stand mixer fitted with paddle attachment, cream butter and brown sugar until light and fluffy, approximately doubled in size.

3. Add eggs one at a time on medium-low speed beating well after each addition. Add vanilla extract in with last egg.

4. Slowly add dry ingredients and beat until batter is just combined.

5. Press dough into bottom of prepared pan. Set aside.

Fudge Filling

1. In medium saucepan, combine butter, sweetened condensed milk, heavy cream, and chocolate chips. Cook over low heat, stirring occasionally, until chocolate melts and mixture is thoroughly combined. Remove from heat and allow to cool slightly.

2. Spread chocolate mixture evenly over blondie base using offset spatula.

Topping

1. Mix together rolled oats, cinnamon, salt, and melted butter in medium bowl to form a crumble.

2. Sprinkle crumble evenly over chocolate layer.

3. Bake bars for 28 minutes, rotating pan halfway through. Bars are done when crumble is lightly browned and chocolate mixture still looks moist.

4. Cool on wire rack completely before removing from pan.

5. Cut into 16 bars – make sure you have a hot pot of coffee ready to go and great friends around to share with!

FOR THE LOVE OF LEMONS LEMON BARS

Yield: 8 lip-smacking bars

I'm not sure there is any sweet treat better suited for summer than lemon bars. Not only is the refreshingly tangy, lip-smacking curd center irresistible, it's extraordinarily rich and buttery crust simply melts in your mouth. With each bite, the combination of the two wakes up your every taste bud, creating the most tempting – tart yet sweet – treat that nobody could resist. Bring these to any summer gathering and you'll find you have quickly become everyone's best friend!

Crust	Preheat oven to 350°F. Coat 8-inch square cake pan with cooking spray and line with parchment.
2.60 oz powdered sugar	Crust
	1. Sift powdered sugar into bowl of stand mixer fitted with paddle attachment.
6.90 oz Shortbread Mix	2. Add Shortbread Mix and beat on low to combine thoroughly.
6 oz butter	3. Add butter and continue to beat on low until dough forms.
Filling	4. Place dough into prepared pan and press evenly into bottom and ½-inch up sides. Dough should be about ¼-inch thick throughout – I like to make mine a little thicker in the corners for good measure.
1.50 oz Shortbread Mix	5. Line dough with parchment and fill with pie weights. Pie weights should fully cover bottom and line all sides and corners. Bake for 16 minutes, rotating pan halfway through. The crust should be light golden brown when done.
12.50 oz sugar	
6 oz fresh lemon juice	Filling
1 lemon, zested	1. While crust is baking, make filling by sifting Shortbread Mix into medium bowl. Add sugar and whisk to combine.
5 eggs	2. Add lemon juice and zest, whisk thoroughly to dissolve sugar. Set aside.
¾ tsp salt	3. In separate bowl, whisk eggs and salt together thoroughly. Then, continue to whisk for an additional 30 seconds.
	4. Slowly stream egg mixture into sugar mixture while whisking. Continue whisking until combined.
Topping	5. When crust is ready, remove pie weights and pour filling directly over hot crust.
QS powdered sugar, sifted	6. Reduce oven temperature to 300°F and bake for approximately 32 minutes until center of custard no longer jiggles. It should look pale yellow in color and contain no brown spots when done.
	7. Let bars cool completely on wire rack. Then cover and refrigerate overnight.
	8. Cut into eight rectangular servings, liberally dust each serving with powdered sugar, and then devour with your best manners possible.

Note: When making filling, do not mix salt with dry ingredients – be sure to whisk with eggs as recipe states.

TANTALIZING TOFFEE CREAM CHEESE BROWNIES

Yield: 16 heavenly bars

I'm often asked what my favorite dessert is, and to be honest, that's a really difficult question to answer. How on earth does one choose? My go to answer is simple: I am a "flavor-of-the-week" kind of gal. I get hooked on a particular sweet treat and eat it every day for weeks on end until one day I crave something new and move on to the next delectable dessert.

However, Tantilizing Toffee Cream Cheese Brownies have always been a mainstay of mine. I love nothing more than to warm one up just a bit in the microwave and then slather on some homemade coffee ice cream. I actually considered this dinner for a while when I first opened the bakery!

I adore these decadent, chewy brownies filled with toffee bits and infused with cream cheese. They always bring a huge smile to my face and make my taste buds jump for joy no matter the occasion. I hope they do just the same for you and yours.

P.S. There are no bowls I love to lick more than those with leftover brownie batter!

Filling

16 oz cream cheese

5 oz sugar

2 eggs

2 Tbsp Cake Mix

Batter

8 oz butter

2.50 oz cocoa powder

5 oz Cake Mix

½ tsp salt

½ tsp baking powder

15 oz sugar

4 eggs, lightly beaten

2 tsp vanilla extract

14.50 oz English toffee bits, divided

Preheat oven to 350°F. Coat 9-by-13-inch cake pan with cooking spray and line with parchment.

Filling

1. In stand mixer fitted with paddle attachment, beat cream cheese and sugar on medium speed until well combined.
2. Add eggs one at a time mixing well after each addition.
3. Add Cake Mix and beat until just combined. Set aside.

Batter + Assembly

1. In large saucepan, melt butter over medium heat. Once melted, remove from heat and let cool for 10 minutes.
2. While butter is cooling, whisk together cocoa powder, Cake Mix, salt, and baking powder in a medium bowl. Set aside.
3. Once butter has cooled slightly, whisk in sugar, eggs, and vanilla extract until combined.
4. Fold in dry ingredients with spatula until combined.
5. Fold in 11.50 ounces of English toffee bits.
6. Pour approximately three-fourths of batter into prepared pan.
7. Using tablespoon, drop cream cheese mixture evenly over batter. Then spoon remaining brownie batter over cream cheese sporadically.
8. Using offset spatula, swirl batter and filling together to form decorative pattern. Tap pan on counter to evenly distribute batter. Then sprinkle remaining English toffee bits over top.
9. Bake for 40 minutes, rotating pan halfway through. Brownies are done when toothpick inserted into center comes out with just a few moist crumbs.
10. Place brownie pan on wire rack to cool slightly before serving.

OLD SCHOOL CARAMELITAS

Yield: 9 magical squares

High school was where it's at! I mean, I'd never go back voluntarily, but I do cherish those years of my life. What I loved more than anything back then were the weekly sleepovers I had with my girlfriends. I doubt I spent a single Friday or Saturday night alone for four years straight.

We'd order pizza, talk about boys, TP our friends' houses, play hide-and-seek on the golf course late at night, and always – without fail – find time to whip up some sort of sweet treat to munch on.

My wonderful, funny, crazy-smart girlfriend Kayla, whom I'm still in touch with today, introduced all of us to Caramelitas back in high school during one of our many sleepovers. She couldn't believe we'd never heard of them! Though we took a few shortcuts in those days using premade chocolate chip cookie dough and caramel from a jar, I'll never forget how delicious those bars were.

A year or two into running the bakery, one batch of chocolate chip cookies was accidentally made with too much flour so I decided not to sell them. However, I didn't want to throw away 200 cookies… and that's when it hit me: Caramelitas! I called up Kayla just to make sure I remembered the recipe correctly and then we turned all of our extra doughy cookie dough into these magical, melt-in-your-mouth cookie bars.

After that, there was no going back! We made Caramelitas at the bakery every single day up until the very last. If you've never had one, stop reading this and start baking now!

---

8 oz salted caramel sauce

28.50 oz chocolate chip cookie dough (or 12 blue scoops)

7 oz milk chocolate chips

Preheat oven to 350°F. Coat 8-inch square cake pan with cooking spray and line with foil.

1. Make one batch of Out-Of-This-World Salted Caramel Sauce (pg. #38). Measure out 8 ounces and set aside. Store remaining sauce in an airtight container and refrigerate for future use – lucky you!

2. Make one batch of Classic Chocolate Chip Cookie Dough (pg. #74). This will be enough for one batch of Caramelitas. Plus, you will have 10 cookies leftover as well for your snacking pleasure!

3. Place 19 ounces (or eight blue scoops) of cookie dough into bottom of prepared pan and press down firmly to form even layer. Parbake dough for 12 minutes.

4. After 12 minutes, remove pan from oven and evenly sprinkle with milk chocolate chips.

5. Slowly pour salted caramel sauce over chocolate. Use offset spatula to smooth caramel evenly over chocolate chips.

6. Break remaining cookie dough into pieces and then smoosh pieces flat. Place flattened pieces randomly over caramel, leaving open spots for caramel to seep through.

7. Return pan to oven and bake for another 18 minutes. Edges of bars should be golden brown and caramel should be slightly bubbly when done. Place pan on wire rack and allow bars to cool to room temperature. Once room temperature, cover and let set overnight.

8. The following day, cut bars into 9 chunky squares and share with only the best of friends!

PURELY CHOCOLATE ROASTED HAZELNUT BROWNIES

Yield: 9 irresistible squares

The creation of these Purely Chocolate Roasted Hazelnut Brownies was TOTALLY a game time decision. I was in the middle of baking all my recipes for the photo shoot of this book when I first thought: NUTELLA® BROWNIES!

How did I never think of these at the bakery? Where was my head at?

I gathered my marbles and sprang into action to whip up my first batch of these brownies that evening after all of my scheduled baking was done for the day, jotting down the recipe as I went along. The first batch of these brownies actually turned out so beautifully that we photographed it for this book!

I've made these countless times since then as they don't seem to last long in our house... probably because I eat one every few hours or so. In any case, be prepared to make a double batch if you plan on sharing because these delicious, indulgent, nutty, bursting-with-chocolate brownies are simply irresistible!

Batter

3.75 oz Cake Mix

1.25 cocoa powder

½ tsp salt

4 oz butter, softened

3.50 oz brown sugar

2 eggs

1 Tbsp vanilla bean paste

15.75 oz chocolate hazelnut spread

Toppings

3.25 oz hazelnuts, roughly chopped

QS sea salt flakes

Preheat oven to 350°F. Coat 8-inch square cake pan with cooking spray and line with parchment.

1. Whisk together Cake Mix, cocoa powder, and salt in medium bowl. Set aside.

2. In stand mixer fitted with paddle attachment, cream butter and brown sugar until light and fluffy, approximately doubled in size.

3. Add eggs one at a time on medium-low speed beating well after each addition. Add vanilla bean paste with last egg.

4. Scrape sides and bottom of bowl. Then, add chocolate hazelnut spread and beat until smooth. Batter will be runny.

5. Slowly add dry ingredients and beat on medium-low until thoroughly combined.

6. Pour batter into prepared pan and bake for 18 minutes.

7. After 18 minutes, remove pan from oven and evenly sprinkle hazelnuts over top. Then, sprinkle with sea salt flakes. Place pan back in oven and bake for another 18 minutes. Brownies are done when toothpick inserted into center comes out with a few moist crumbs.

8. Let cool on wire rack to room temperature before removing brownies from pan. Once removed, cut into 9 squares and serve warm with overflowing cups of milk.

COULDN'T-BE-MORE-PERFECT PECAN PIE BARS

Yield: 16 richly delicious bars

You know when you go to someone's house for dinner and you're asked to bring a dish, be it a salad, or dip, or just a bag of chips, and you really don't care if you come home with the leftovers? Well, these Couldn't-Be-More-Perfect Pecan Pie Bars are indeed the BEST dish to bring to any get together, but, as I've learned, are not that easy to leave behind...

First things first, I made sure I left a few bars at home as I already knew I couldn't survive without them. Then, by the time I got to the get together, I had thought more about it and realized I probably didn't leave enough at home. So there I was, in the car, discretely removing some bars from the tray and stashing them away in my glove box. I then reorganized the platter to make it look full again before entering the gathering. By the time dessert rolled around – I'd had even more time to think – and decided it was best to not only eat a Pecan Pie Bar at the party but also wrap one up in a napkin to take home or perhaps eat in the car, whichever came first.

I have been in this position several times now and I am not ashamed whatsoever. These ooey, gooey, buttery, sweet-and-salty, rich, and delicious pecan pie bars are utterly irresistible! My recommendation is to bake a double batch while wearing sweatpants.

Crust

Preheat oven to 350°F. Coat 9-by-13-inch cake pan with cooking spray and line with foil.

8 oz butter, softened

Crust

5.25 oz brown sugar

1. In stand mixer fitted with paddle attachment, cream together butter and brown sugar until light and fluffy, approximately doubled in size.

11.80 oz Shortbread Mix

2. Add Shortbread Mix and salt. Beat on medium-low speed until crumbly dough forms.

½ tsp salt

3. Press dough into prepared pan and bake for 20 minutes, rotating pan halfway through. Crust should be light golden brown when done.

Filling

Filling

8 oz butter

1. While crust bakes, prepare filling by combining butter, brown sugar, honey, and heavy cream in medium saucepan. Stir constantly over medium heat until mixture is thoroughly combined and begins to thicken. Cook mixture for one more minute and then remove from heat.

12 oz brown sugar

8 oz honey

2. Stir in chopped pecans with spatula.

2 oz heavy cream

3. Remove crust from oven when ready and immediately pour pecan filling over hot crust. Use offset spatula to spread filling evenly over crust.

16 oz pecans, medium chopped

4. Return pan to oven and bake an additional 20 minutes.

5. Remove pan from oven and place on wire rack to cool completely.

6. Once cool, sprinkle bars with sea salt flakes and then transfer to a cutting board. Peel off foil and cut up to share.

Topping

P.S. These bars will fly out of your house faster than you think. Be sure to set some aside for a little bit of "me time". Afterall, *you* made them and *you* should get to savor at least one bar in peace!

QS sea salt flakes

SENSATIONAL SWEET POTATO PIE BARS

Yield: 8 brilliant bars

When I was going to culinary school in Boston I was also a part-time nanny for a family. They were a kind, generous, and loving family with two absolutely adorable kids. One year, my then boyfriend and I decided to stay in Boston for Thanksgiving and celebrate just the two of us. Flights home were expensive and we'd both being going home for Christmas so it didn't seem like a big deal.

Just three days before Thanksgiving, my boyfriend informed me he booked a flight home for Thanksgiving... just one flight... for himself. Insert enormous amount of awkward silence. In any case, this left me alone in our apartment – mad as hell – baking pies and gulping red wine.

When the Carters found out what had happened, they immediately invited me over for Thanksgiving. Since I didn't quite feel like being alone, I quickly agreed. Their family took me in as if I had been one of them for years – it reminded me so much of the way my parents always took in stragglers over the holidays. The house was filled with a magical energy – a combination of true laughter, unconditional love, sweet and savory aromas from the kitchen, and kids playing like there was no tomorrow. It was perfect.

To add the cherry on top, the Carters prepared an exceptional Southern Thanksgiving dinner. Most of it I could eat but there were a few things I couldn't, including the one item I wanted most: Sweet Potato Pie.

Six years after that Thanksgiving, I created my Sensational Sweet Potato Pie Bars. We had a lot of pies going out at the bakery so I wanted to do something a little different. These bars still have all the fall spices - think cinnamon, nutmeg, and allspice - that sweet potato pies traditionally do, but are put in a league of their own with their homemade graham cracker crust and brilliantly burnt meringue topping. I'd like to think that if the Carters ever tried these Sensational Sweet Potato Pie Bars, they'd not only love them, but would invite me back for another Thanksgiving.

Crust

10.25 oz graham crackers

2.80 oz sugar

½ tsp cinnamon

4 oz butter, melted

Filling

16 oz sweet potato

1.75 oz brown sugar

3 eggs

1 tsp salt

1½ tsp cinnamon

¾ tsp allspice

¼ tsp nutmeg

2 Tbsp bourbon

8 oz whole milk

4 oz heavy cream

4.25 oz sour cream

Meringue Topping

7.50 oz sugar

4 oz water

4 egg whites, room temperature

½ tsp cream of tartar

Preheat oven to 350°F. Coat 8-inch square cake pan with cooking spray and line with foil.

Crust

1. Make one batch of Homemade Honey Graham Crackers (pg. #84) or buy premade gluten free graham crackers from the store.

2. Place graham crackers in food processor and pulse until a fine crumb forms. Place crumbs into large bowl.

3. Add sugar, cinnamon, and melted butter; stir to combine.

4. Pour crust into prepared pan and press down into even layer using hands. Bake crust for five minutes and then let cool completely on wire rack before adding filling.

Filling

1. Microwave sweet potato on high for approximately 8 minutes until tender. When ready, remove from microwave using tongs, towel, or oven mitts and let cool slightly. Then, remove peel and cut potato into 1-inch wide circles. Place sweet potato in bowl of stand mixer fitted with paddle attachment and beat on medium speed until smooth.

2. Add brown sugar and beat until well incorporated.

3. Add eggs one at a time, beating well after each addition.

4. Add remaining ingredients, from salt to sour cream, and beat on low until thoroughly combined.

5. Pour filling over cooled crust. If needed, level with offset spatula.

6. Bake for 1 hour, rotating pan halfway through. Bars are done when outer edges have browned slightly and filling has puffed up. Center may still be a little wobbly and that's okay. Remove pan from oven and let cool on wire rack to room temperature. Cover and refrigerate overnight to set.

Meringue Topping (Made Next Day)

1. Remove bars from pan and place on cutting board. Cut bars into eight rectangles and place back in refrigerator until meringue is ready. I like to cut bars first as Italian Meringue can be pretty sticky to cut through.

2. In small saucepan over high heat, combine sugar and water. Cook until syrup reaches 240°F on candy thermometer. If water bursts up sides of pan, brush it off using a silicon pastry brush and clean water.

3. While sugar is cooking, place egg whites and cream of tartar in bowl of stand mixer fitted with whisk attachment. Whisk on medium speed until soft peaks form; takes approximately 2 to 3 minutes.

4. Once sugar has reached 240°F, adjust mixer to low and slowly pour in hot syrup. Be careful, syrup may fly out if it hits the whisk. Once all syrup is added, adjust mixer to high and whip until meringue is stiff and glossy.

5. Meringue is now ready to pipe on bars. This can be done several different ways. First, place meringue in piping bag fitted with medium plain tip and pipe Hershey®-Kiss-like designs on top. A star tip can be used for more intricate details. A scoop also works great here – scoop meringue onto bars and then slightly flatten with offset spatula. Or, simply dollop meringue on bars with spoon and use offset spatula to give meringue texture. There is no right or wrong way and they all taste delicious!

6. To finish bars, use kitchen torch to toast meringue. Meringue will pop up, adding height and a dramatic flare to bars! Eat immediately! I'm only joking; meringue can sit in refrigerator for 24 to 48 hours as long as it is kept in an airtight container.

SIMPLY MAGIC, MAGIC BARS

Yield: 16 to-die-for bars

Growing up we had a lot of traditions surrounding Christmas. We knew Christmas Eve would always be held at Oma and Opa's. Rouladen would be served as well as Glüwein. We would definitely sing Christmas songs as a family regardless of how awful we all sounded. The kids would put on a talent show before gifts were opened and my Aunt would always give everyone a package of homemade snack mix and her delectable magic bars.

I loved her magic bars. I truly thought they made her a magician in the kitchen. Every year I was so excited to get my portion and devoured them as soon as I could possibly imagine eating again – I was often far too stuffed after Christmas dinner to even think about dessert! When I became Celiac and could no longer eat her perfect magic bars, I knew I had to create my own.

These Simply Magic, Magic Bars are one of the easiest recipes in this book, but don't underestimate them. The toasted nuts, variety of chocolates, cinnamon, and coconut naturally create such complex flavors that you can just sit back and wait for your timer to buzz. Follow the recipe and you'll end up with dessert bars so delicious, you'd think a professional pastry chef was in your kitchen!

Crust

11 oz graham crackers

6.50 oz shredded coconut

¼ tsp cinnamon

8 oz butter, melted

Toppings

14 oz sweetened condensed milk

3.75 oz walnuts, toasted and roughly chopped

3.75 oz pecans, toasted and roughly chopped

8.50 oz dark chocolate chunks

5.50 oz white chocolate chips

5.50 oz butterscotch chips

Preheat oven to 300°F. Coat 9-by-13-inch cake pan with cooking spray and line with parchment.

1. Make one batch of Homemade Honey Graham Crackers (pg. #84) or buy premade gluten free graham crackers from the store.

2. Place graham crackers in food processor and pulse until a fine crumb forms. Place crumbs into large bowl.

3. Add coconut, cinnamon, and melted butter; stir to combine.

4. Scoop crust into prepared pan and press down into even layer using hands. Refrigerate for 15 minutes to allow butter to firm up and then bake for 10 minutes or until golden brown.

5. Let cool on wire rack for 10 minutes before topping with filling. Increase oven temperature to 325°F.

6. Slowly pour sweetened condensed milk over crust; it is okay if crust is still warm. Use offset spatula to spread condensed milk evenly over crust.

7. Sprinkle half of walnuts and half of pecans evenly over sweetened condensed milk.

8. Sprinkle chocolate chunks, white chocolate chips, and butterscotch chips over nuts.

9. Sprinkle remaining nuts over entire mixture.

10. Bake bars for 22 minutes, rotating pan halfway through. Toppings should be golden brown and bubbly around edges when done. Transfer pan to wire rack and let cool completely before cutting.

11. These bars can be a bit messy to cut. A sharp (non-serrated) knife works best and the bigger the bars, the better!

COPYCAT GINGER BERRY BARS

Yield: 16 dreamy bars

The first year RylieCakes was open for the holidays I got loads of requests for Starbucks® Cranberry Bliss Bars. The only problem was, I had never tried them! Oat Fudge Bars were my go to at Starbucks® – I had never paid the Cranberry Bliss Bars any attention. I'm a die-hard chocolate fan, what can I say?

So when it came to recreating a treat I've never had, I decided to go out, buy a few, cut them up, and have everyone else try them and tell me everything! Meanwhile, I broke apart a bar of my own, gaining a feel for the texture of the cake and frosting. Having taken enough notes, I went to the World Wide Web to peruse a few other copycat recipes. I was on the right path and ready to whip these puppies up.

I immediately knew what all of the fuss was about when I bit into my first bar – they were absolutely dreamy. At the bakery we ended up calling them Ginger Berry Bars and sold them year round as they were such a big hit each and every day. Now you too can enjoy these Copycat Ginger Berry Bars whenever you want, wherever you want!

Batter

7.50 oz Cake Mix

¼ tsp xanthan gum

½ tsp baking powder

¼ tsp salt

6 oz butter, softened

8.75 oz brown sugar

3 eggs

1 tsp vanilla extract

1 tsp orange extract

2 oz crystallized ginger, finely chopped

3.50 oz dried cranberries, roughly chopped

4 oz white chocolate chips

Frosting

6 oz cream cheese, softened

10.60 oz powdered sugar, sifted

1 tsp vanilla extract

1 tsp orange zest

Icing

2.25 oz powdered sugar

1 Tbsp milk

Topping

QS dried cranberries, roughly chopped

Preheat oven to 350°F. Coat 9-by-13-inch cake pan with cooking spray and line with parchment.

Batter

1. Whisk together Cake Mix, xanthan gum, baking powder, and salt in medium bowl. Set aside.

2. In stand mixer fitted with paddle attachment, cream butter and brown sugar until light and fluffy, approximately doubled in size.

3. On medium-low speed, add eggs one at a time, beating well after each addition. Add both extracts with last egg.

4. Slowly add dry ingredients and beat on low until smooth.

5. Mix in chopped ginger, dried cranberries, and white chocolate chips. Continue to beat on low until just incorporated.

6. Pour batter into prepared pan and bake for 22 minutes, rotating pan halfway through. Top of bars should be light golden brown when done. Remove from oven and let cool on wire rack.

Frosting

1. While bars are cooling, mix together cream cheese, powdered sugar, vanilla extract, and orange zest in stand mixer fitted with paddle attachment. Beat until smooth.

2. When bars have cooled to room temperature, use offset spatula to spread frosting evenly over top.

Drizzle Icing + Topping

1. Whisk together powdered sugar and milk in small bowl. If icing is too thick, add more milk. If icing is too runny, add more powdered sugar.

2. To decorate with icing, there are two techniques to choose from. First, spoon icing into piping bag – or re-sealable sandwich bag – and cut a tiny hole at tip. Move your wrist in large zigzag motions across the bars while applying pressure to bag to create a beautiful design. The second option is a bit less technical; simply grab a spoon and splatter icing on bars to create a more fun, artistic design. Whichever method you choose, your bars will be fabulous!

3. Last but not least, sprinkle bars with dried cranberries before cutting, serving, and thanking yourself for making such a magical treat.

Note: In place of icing, you can use melted white chocolate for drizzle. It dries hard and adds a little crunch to every bite!

breakfast bites

THE ORIGINAL RYLIECAKES RECIPE: QUINOA BANANA BREAD

Yield: 8 magical mini loaves

In my early twenties I moved to Tempe, AZ, to enroll myself in a specialty pain clinic. I was chasing a cure for chronic pain and a bunch of other wild symptoms I'd been experiencing since I was 14.

I didn't know a soul in Arizona. I was transferring from a school of nearly 2,000 students to ASU that had almost 60,000 students, I spent many of my afternoons in doctor's appointments, and I was withdrawing from several heavy medications that I had been on for far too long. Needless to say, I was depressed. I was, however, lucky enough to have three things pulling me through each and every day: my dog Apple, my good friend Charles, and baking.

It was in Tempe that I started to play around with my own flour mixes and began writing some recipes. This Quinoa Banana Bread was, in fact, my first recipe. I remember making these over and over and over again trying to perfect them. Charles would always cheerfully help me gobble up the botched batches. After I finally perfected them, he and I would eat them before yoga (not our best idea), after yoga, for breakfast, for dessert, and anytime in between! Not unexpectedly, they quickly became a staple at the bakery.

Every time I bake these, the aroma gets the best of me. They have a lovely way of making the air smell sweet and cinnamony. And whenever I begin munching on my own mini loaf, I always think of Charles' charming smile and a funny friendship that brightened even my darkest days.

3.25 oz walnuts

10 oz Cake Mix

1 tsp baking soda

1 tsp salt

2 tsp cinnamon

3 large bananas

1 egg

2 oz maple syrup

1 tsp vanilla extract

5.25 oz brown sugar

4.75 oz cooked quinoa

5.75 oz semi-sweet chocolate chips

Preheat oven to 350°F. Coat 8-cavity mini loaf pan with cooking spray.

1. Line rimmed baking sheet with parchment, place walnuts in single layer on parchment. Bake in preheated oven for 7 to 10 minutes until golden brown and have a nutty fragrance. Remove from oven, cool completely, and then roughly chop. Turn oven down to 325°F.

2. Whisk together Cake Mix, baking soda, salt, and cinnamon in medium bowl. Set aside.

3. In bowl of stand mixer fitted with paddle attachment, beat bananas on medium speed until they start to look soupy with only a few chunks remaining.

4. Add egg and beat until combined.

5. Adjust mixer to medium-low, add maple syrup, vanilla extract, brown sugar, and cooked quinoa. Beat until just combined.

6. Add dry ingredients and beat on low until combined.

7. Add chocolate chips and chopped walnuts and beat until just combined.

8. Portion batter evenly among all 8 cavities; an ivory scoop works perfect here.

9. Bake for 36 minutes, rotating pan halfway through. Loaves are done when golden brown and toothpick inserted into center comes out clean. Place pan on wire rack to cool.

Note: These mini loaves are best warm. If you are not eating straight from the oven, consider microwaving a few seconds so that the chocolate melts in your mouth every time!

ALL GROWN-UP ALMOND POPPYSEED MUFFINS

Yield: 12 marvelous muffins

When I was a kid I absolutely loved to stay the night at my best friend's house. Okay, who didn't?! That was a silly statement. Let me start over…

When I was a kid I loved waking up at my best friend Brenda's house for breakfast. Her mom actually bought Costco muffins! This might sound crazy, but you would never find such a thing at our house, so it truly was a treat. These muffins were huge, loaded with sugar, moist, and mouthwatering. The cherry on top of all this goodness was that Pam, Brenda's mom, would slice 'em up for us and serve us at the table! Breakfast at Brenda's never let you down.

After going gluten free, I constantly craved almond poppyseed muffins but I was consistently disappointed by all the ones I got my hands on. When we created this recipe at RylieCakes Bakery, my heart instantly melted. It was love at first bite. These muffins were everything I had been missing and more: light, fluffy, and sweet with a crunch of toasted almonds and a dusting of caramelized sugar on top. A moment of true pastry perfection that brought me right back to my sweet, sweet childhood.

12.50 oz Cake Mix

2 tsp baking powder

½ tsp salt

10 oz sugar

2 eggs

8 oz canola oil

5.50 oz buttermilk

2 tsp vanilla extract

1½ tsp almond extract

8.50 oz sour cream

1½ Tbsp poppy seeds

3.50 oz slivered almonds

QS sparkling sugar

Preheat oven to 375°F. Place 12 parchment liners in standard 12-cup muffin pan.

1. Whisk together Cake Mix, baking powder, and salt in medium bowl. Set aside.

2. In stand mixer fitted with paddle attachment, beat sugar, eggs, oil, buttermilk, and both extracts on low speed until well combined.

3. Add dry ingredients and beat until incorporated.

4. Add sour cream and poppy seeds, beat until just combined. Scrape down sides and bottom of bowl with spatula.

5. Portion batter evenly among liners; a grey scoop works perfect here. Top each with slivered almonds and sprinkle liberally with sparkling sugar.

6. Bake for 30 minutes, rotating pan halfway through. Muffins are done when toothpick inserted into center comes out clean; a few clinging crumbs are okay.

7. Allow muffins to cool slightly in pan before diving in!

MELT-IN-YOUR-MOUTH CHOCOLATE SOUR CREAM MUFFINS

Yield: 12 sensational muffins

While working at the bakery, my life could easily be described in two words: organized chaos. I worked early mornings, late nights, weekends, and everything in between. Occasionally I would squeeze in a day off during the week. My days off were essentially one of two scenarios.

Scenario 1: I'd sleep in with our fur babies until my little heart desired – Barkley and Oliver loved to sleep in. We'd then all get up and move to the couch where we'd cuddle some more and drink cup after cup of black coffee while browsing through foodie magazines. Eventually, I'd make a huge bowl of Garlic Parmesan Popcorn, pour myself a mug of wine, and then hop in a bubble bath where I would watch scandalous TV shows like Scandal or The Good Wife. Finally, I'd ask Ben to pick up food on the way home so I could successfully continue doing nothing.

Scenario 2: I'd pop out of bed ready to rumble, the energizer bunny in me running at full speed ahead! I'd fill my day with baking, cooking, recipe testing, cleaning, running errands, doing house chores, yoga, paddle boarding, walking Barkley, yada yada yada.

As you might guess, it was a Scenario 2 kind of day that these muffins were created. As soon as they popped out of the oven, I put half a dozen in a darling little picnic basket and headed over to Ben's work. Ben and I sat in the sun on the bed of his truck and each enjoyed more than one oven-fresh muffin while sipping hot coffee. It was a glorious way to start the day.

8.50 oz Cake Mix

3.50 oz cocoa powder

2½ tsp baking powder

½ tsp baking soda

½ tsp salt

2 eggs

2 egg yolks

8.75 oz sugar

4 oz coconut oil, melted

12 oz sour cream

1 Tbsp vanilla extract

12 oz dark chocolate chips, divided

QS sea salt

Preheat oven to 350°F. Place 12 parchment liners in standard 12-cup muffin pan.

1. Whisk together Cake Mix, cocoa powder, baking powder, baking soda, and salt in medium bowl. Set aside.

2. In bowl of stand mixer fitted with whisk attachment, whisk eggs and egg yolks on medium-high speed. Once combined, slowly add sugar and whisk mixture until thick and pale yellow in color.

3. Adjust mixer to medium, pour coconut oil slowly into batter and whisk until thoroughly incorporated. Though coconut oil should be melted here, it should not be hot. Make sure coconut oil has had time to cool after melting.

4. Add sour cream and vanilla extract and whisk until combined. Scrape down sides and bottom of bowl with spatula.

5. Add dry ingredients and 10 ounces of chocolate chips. Whisk on low until just combined.

6. Portion batter evenly among liners; an ivory scoop works perfect here. Sprinkle remaining 2 ounces of chocolate chips on top of muffins.

7. Bake for 28 minutes, rotating pan halfway through. Muffins are done when toothpick inserted into center comes out clean; a few clinging crumbs are okay.

8. Immediately after removing from oven, sprinkle muffins with sea salt. To each their own here, but I personally like more salt! Allow muffins to cool slightly before chowing down.

THE ULTIMATE PUMPKIN MUFFINS

Yield: 15 mind-blowing muffins

I had a hard time naming these muffins. What do you call a muffin that has everything?

These muffins are made up of a rich, cinnamon batter that has you dreaming of your favorite pumpkin pie until you get a bite of those toasted pecans...Then your mind travels to that buttery, nutty place we all love to go in fall until BAM! Your lips meet the tangy, creamy, sensational filling packed with a punch of orange zest. You finally swallow your first (overly generous) bite and are greeted with hints of caramelized sugar from the slightly candied pecan nestled on top. The only thing that could possibly make these muffins better is if you ate them in an enormous, cozy sweater by a crackling, festive, house-warming fire.

So, after all of that thought, I knew these must be The Ultimate Pumpkin Muffins.

Filling

12 oz cream cheese

3 Tbsp Cake Mix

3.75 oz sugar

1 egg

1 Tbsp orange zest

Batter

4.25 oz pecans

17 oz Cake Mix

2 tsp baking soda

1½ tsp cinnamon

½ tsp salt

16 oz canned pumpkin

8 oz canola oil

4 eggs

2 egg yolks

18.75 oz sugar

3.50 oz brown sugar

Topping

15 whole pecans

QS sparkling sugar

Preheat oven to 375°F. Place 15 parchment liners in two standard 12-cup muffin pans.

Filling

1. In stand mixer fitted with paddle attachment, beat cream cheese and Cake Mix until smooth.

2. Slowly add sugar and mix until well incorporated.

3. Add egg and orange zest. Beat until thoroughly combined. Set aside.

Batter

1. Line rimmed baking sheet with parchment, place pecans in single layer on parchment. Bake in preheated oven for 5 to 7 minutes until golden brown and have a nutty fragrance. Remove from oven, cool completely, and then roughly chop.

2. Whisk together Cake Mix, baking soda, cinnamon, and salt in medium bowl. Set aside.

3. In stand mixer fitted with paddle attachment, beat together pumpkin, oil, eggs, egg yolks, and both sugars on medium-low speed.

4. Add dry ingredients and beat until incorporated.

5. Add chopped pecans and mix until just combined.

6. Portion batter evenly among liners; a grey scoop works perfect here.

7. Using black scoop (or tablespoon), portion filling on top of each muffin. Filling will slightly sink into batter.

8. Top each muffin with 1 whole pecan and generously sprinkle with sparkling sugar.

9. Bake muffins for 28 minutes, rotating pan halfway through. Muffins are done when toothpick inserted into center comes out clean; a few clinging crumbs are okay.

10. Allow muffins to cool slightly before gobbling them all up one by one.

P.S. These muffins pair perfectly with a slow-sipping glass of drier, spicier bourbon. Enjoy!

SWEET + SALTY SPICED APPLE MUFFINS

Yield: 17 loaded muffins

These Sweet + Salty Spiced Apple Muffins originally started out as a cake. The cake version was three layers of heavenly spiced cake with moist chunks of apple politely interrupting every bite, separated by none other than a decadent salted caramel sauce. To finish it off, the cake was smothered inside and out with a classic Vanilla Bean Swiss Meringue Buttercream. The cake was prize worthy – truly a masterpiece. However, one slice of this bad boy could very well put you in a food coma for days.

So we started offering the cake in the form of cupcakes, sheet cakes, and even came up with a vegan version. After watching each and every version we made this combination in fly off the shelves, I decided to rework the recipe a little. I was hoping to transform this amazing cake into a breakfast muffin must-have.

The transformation was clearly a success as these muffins worked their way right into my first cookbook. These wildly decadent, seriously loaded muffins satisfy both your sweet and salty side... Never mind the calories!

Batter

9 oz Honeycrisp apple, grated

10.60 oz Cake Mix

5 oz Roux Mix

1 tsp baking powder

1 tsp baking soda

1 tsp salt

1 tsp ground ginger

½ tsp allspice

7.50 oz sugar

6.75 oz brown sugar

10 oz canola oil

4 eggs

8.50 oz goat cheese, divided

Crumble Topping

1.75 oz rolled oats

1.25 oz Cake Mix

1.20 oz brown sugar

1.25 oz sugar

½ tsp cinnamon

¼ tsp salt

¼ tsp allspice

1 oz butter, melted

Apple Topping

8 oz Honeyscrisp apple, small diced

3 oz butter

5.25 oz brown sugar

1.5 tsp cinnamon

129

Preheat oven to 375°F. Place 17 parchment liners into two standard 12-cup muffin pans.

Crumble Topping

1. Whisk together all ingredients except butter. Once thoroughly combined, slowly pour in melted butter and fold mixture until incorporated. Set aside.

Batter

1. Using box grater, grate apples and pat dry with paper towels to soak up as much juice as possible. Set aside.

2. Whisk together Cake Mix, Roux Mix, baking powder, baking soda, salt, ginger, and allspice in medium bowl. Set aside.

3. In stand mixer fitted with paddle attachment, beat together both sugars, oil, and eggs on medium speed until thoroughly combined.

4. Add dry ingredients and beat until incorporated.

5. Adjusting mixer to low, add grated apple and mix until just combined.

6. Portion batter evenly among liners; an ivory scoop works perfect here.

7. Add half an ounce of goat cheese to top of each muffin. It will slightly sink into batter and that's just what you want!

8. Bake muffins for 12 minutes. Then remove muffins from oven and quickly sprinkle crumble topping over each muffin. Bake for another 8 minutes. Muffins are done when toothpick inserted into center comes out clean; a few clinging crumbs are okay.

Apple Topping

1. While muffins are baking, place small sauté pan over medium heat and add all Apple Topping ingredients. Cook until butter and sugar start to caramelize and apples soften; it takes just a few minutes.

2. Immediately after removing muffins from oven, spoon apple topping over muffins. Allow muffins to cool slightly before chowing down while they're still nice and warm.

P.S. I like to sprinkle more goat cheese on top of each muffin!

SERIOUSLY MARVELOUS BLUEBERRY MUFFINS

Yield: 12 marvelous muffins

In the beginning, RylieCakes Bakery had a really hard time selling muffins. Partially, I thought, it was because we opened at an "off-muffin" hour at 10 AM. Now, I don't know about you, but I associate muffins with breakfast – all that sweet, light, fluffy, cakey-ness filled with nuts and berries and topped with absurd amounts of sugar and crumble equated to a well-rounded breakfast in my world. Breakfast for me took place between the hours of 4 AM and 9 AM with several cups of hot coffee; 10 AM just didn't seem like the time to eat a muffin.

Furthermore, we were constantly altering our recipe, trying to find one that customers loved. Unfortunately, you change a recipe a few times over and customers stop buying muffins altogether because they never know what they are going to get! Fair enough.

But then one day a miracle happened. We produced the most magical blueberry muffin of all. Customers were now buying ALL of the muffins instead of just one or two and they were buying them morning, noon, and night. A few customers even said that they were the best blueberry muffins they had ever had, with or without gluten!

Drum roll please... I proudly introduce to you the recipe for these Seriously Marvelous Blueberry Muffins.

12.50 oz Cake Mix

2 tsp baking powder

½ tsp salt

10 oz sugar

2 eggs

8 oz canola oil

5.25 oz buttermilk

1 Tbsp vanilla extract

8.50 oz sour cream

13.75 oz blueberries, divided

QS sparkling sugar

Preheat oven to 375°F. Place 12 parchment liners in standard 12-cup muffin pan.

1. Whisk together Cake Mix, baking powder, and salt in medium bowl. Set aside.

2. In stand mixer fitted with paddle attachment, beat sugar, eggs, oil, buttermilk, and vanilla extract on low until well combined.

3. Add dry ingredients and beat until just incorporated.

4. Add sour cream and beat until combined.

5. Fold 10.75 ounces blueberries into batter with spatula.

6. Portion batter evenly among liners; a grey scoop works perfect here. Top each with remaining blueberries and sprinkle liberally with sparkling sugar.

7. Bake muffins for 30 minutes, rotating pan halfway through. Muffins are done when toothpick inserted into center comes out clean; a few clinging crumbs are okay.

8. Allow muffins to cool slightly before gobbling right up with a hot cup of coffee or tea.

Note: Add fresh lemon zest in Step #5 to brighten muffins flavor profile.

OMA'S LEMON RICOTTA CAKELETTES

Yield: 8 Oma-approved cakelettes

My Oma has always been one of my biggest fans, tirelessly supporting me through all of my endeavors in life. And though incredibly kind, sweet, and caring, she is also shamelessly blunt. When recipe testing my new creations, Oma would always be the first to say she likes it but doesn't love it. Perhaps it is too sweet, not salty enough, or plainly missing something. One time she even called me up to go over a list of items I could work on! HA! Some might take offense to this but it was how I grew up – it was as natural to me as waking up in the morning.

The good thing about Oma's fierce approach to life was that when she gave you a compliment, you knew you nailed it! Oma is not the type to hand out compliments easily. An Oma compliment was sincerely genuine every single time.

So when Oma tried these Lemon Ricotta Cakelettes for the first time and said, "They are perfect! My new favorite, I will order some to keep in the house. When will you make them again?". I knew RylieCakes had another flawless pastry to add to its repertoire.

---

6 oz almond flour

3 oz Cake Mix

4.25 oz butter, softened

8.50 oz powdered sugar, divided

1 Tbsp vanilla bean paste

1 tsp almond extract

2 lemons, zested

4 eggs, separated

2 egg yolks

10.50 oz ricotta

QS slivered almonds

QS powdered sugar

Preheat oven to 375°F. Place 8 crumb cake liners on half-sheet pan.

This recipe calls for two stand mixers or one stand mixer and one hand mixer. It is very important to *mise en place* this recipe to ensure accurate timing on all steps.

1. Whisk together almond flour and Cake Mix in small bowl. Set aside.

2. In stand mixer fitted with paddle attachment, cream together butter, half of powdered sugar, vanilla bean paste, almond extract, and lemon zest. When done, mixture should be light and fluffy, approximately doubled in size. See step #6 to ensure egg whites are whisking simultaneously.

3. Add all 6 yolks one at a time, beating well between each addition.

4. Add dry ingredients and beat until just combined.

5. Fold in ricotta with spatula. Be sure to incorporate batter from very bottom and sides of mixing bowl.

6. While creaming butter (see step #2), in separate mixing bowl fitted with whisk attachment, whisk all 6 egg whites and remaining powdered sugar until stiff peaks form. A hand mixer with balloon whisk attachment also works here.

7. When both parts are ready, fold half of meringue from step #6 into batter with spatula – again, incorporating batter from bottom and sides of bowl. Gently fold in remaining meringue.

8. Portion batter evenly among liners; a white scoop works perfect here.

9. Bake for 22 minutes and then remove from oven. Sprinkle slivered almonds over cakelettes – I use approximately 2 tablespoons each. Place back in oven and bake another 10 minutes. Place pan on wire rack and let cool.

10. Once cool, sprinkle with powdered sugar and dig in!

NO FUSS DONUT HOLES

Yield: 28 tasty donut holes

My nanny and grandpa used to come over every Sunday after their church service with a huge box of donuts. Woodi, my brother, was in heaven. He loved all the donuts! The ones with powdered sugar and those covered in cinnamon sugar, the chocolate glazed ones, the crème filled ones, the marble frosting ones, and the maple glazed ones. He adored the donuts filled with jelly and just the good old-fashioned, classic glazed donuts. I, on the other hand, disliked each and every one of them. Seriously, I'm not sure I ever ate a donut in its entirety in my whole life.

After dozens of requests for some kind of donut at RylieCakes, we finally gave in and started making donut holes. It was then, that I went from never eating donuts ever–ever–ever, to gobbling down donut holes in one bite. Honestly, I'd eat them directly out of the fryer, right after they were rolled in cinnamon-sugar, and I'd gobble up any leftovers remaining after the morning rush. Who knew donuts could be so good?

Batter

12.50 oz Cake Mix

2 oz sugar

1½ Tbsp cinnamon

2 tsp turmeric

1 Tbsp baking powder

2 eggs

6 oz milk

1 tsp vanilla extract

2 oz butter, melted

QS canola oil for frying

Toppings

7.50 oz sugar + 1 oz cinnamon

4.25 oz powdered sugar

Prep fryer with oil and set to 350°F. I use a Cuisinart Compact 1.1 Liter Deep Fryer. You can also heat oil in heavy skillet over stove. If using the latter method, do not heat up oil until ready to fry.

1. Whisk together Cake Mix, sugar, cinnamon, turmeric, and baking powder in medium bowl. Set aside.

2. In stand mixer fitted with paddle attachment, beat together eggs, milk, vanilla extract, and melted butter on medium speed for 2 minutes.

3. Add dry ingredients, adjust mixer to medium-high and beat for 4 more minutes.

4. Scrape sides and bottom of bowl with spatula. Cover batter and refrigerate for at least 20 minutes. Resting batter before frying is important, do not skip this step! You can also make batter the day before and refrigerate overnight.

5. While batter is resting, set up cooling area next to fryer by placing wire rack on top of sheet of foil.

6. To fry donut holes, use purple scoop (or tablespoon) to drop 5 to 6 balls of batter into fryer at a time. Fry for 4 minutes and then remove from fryer with slotted spoon and place on wire rack. If donut holes are not frying evenly on all sides, gently rotate them halfway through frying using slotted spoon.

7. Continue to fry donut holes in batches until batter is gone.

8. If rolling in cinnamon-sugar mixture, do so while donut holes are still hot – more cinnamon-sugar will stick to them! If rolling in powdered sugar, wait until donut holes have cooled slightly. Rolling a hot donut hole in powdered sugar creates a sticky mess. Or simply enjoy them plain; it is totally up to you!

Note: Donut holes are best fresh from the fryer.

JUST GOOD OL' FASHIONED COFFEE CAKE

Yield: 10 generous slices

When I first decided to put coffee cake on the menu at RylieCakes I whole-heartedly believed it needed a better name. To me, Coffee Cake seemed to be old-fashioned and boring. So with the help of my staff in a brainstorming session, we renamed this cake "Coffee-Pecan Crumble Cake". And then, "Cinnamon-Pecan Crumble Cake" and then, "Pecan-Cinnamon Coffee Crumble Cake" and then, "Toasted Pecan Coffee Crumble Cake" and then… totally kidding! I only renamed it four times.

The cake was so incredibly scrumptious – all I wanted was for the whole wide world to enjoy it! I just couldn't get the name right. Finally, one day I just said "F*&$ it!" and called it coffee cake. Just Good Ol' Fashioned Coffee Cake. And lo and behold, it sold like crazy! Some things should never change; coffee cake will always be a classic.

Crumble Topping

1.50 oz pecans

4 oz brown sugar

1.80 oz rolled oats

1.50 oz coconut oil, melted

¾ tsp cinnamon

Filling

4 oz pecans

1.75 oz brown sugar

½ tsp cinnamon

Cake

10 oz Cake Mix

1¼ tsp baking powder

½ tsp baking soda

½ tsp salt

4 oz butter, softened

7.50 oz sugar

2 eggs

1 egg yolk

1½ tsp vanilla extract

8.50 oz sour cream

Icing

2.25 oz powdered sugar

1 Tbsp milk

Preheat oven to 350°F. Coat 9.50-inch angel food cake pan with cooking spray and set upside down on a sheet of parchment until ready to use.

Crumble Topping

1. Line rimmed baking sheet with parchment, place pecans (for crumble topping and filling) in single layer on parchment. Bake in preheated oven for 7 to 10 minutes until golden brown and have a nutty fragrance. Remove from oven, cool completely, and then roughly chop.

2. In small bowl, whisk together brown sugar, rolled oats, coconut oil, cinnamon, and 1.50 ounces toasted pecans. Set aside.

Filling

1. In small bowl, mix together brown sugar, cinnamon, and remaining 4 ounces pecans. Refrigerate until ready to use.

Cake

1. Sift Cake Mix, baking powder, baking soda, and salt into medium bowl. Whisk thoroughly and set aside.

2. In stand mixer fitted with paddle attachment, cream butter and sugar until light and fluffy, approximately doubled in size. Scrape down sides and bottom of bowl.

3. Beat in eggs and egg yolk one at a time until incorporated. Add vanilla extract with last egg.

4. Add half the dry ingredients and beat on low speed until just combined. Add sour cream and beat again until just combined. Add remaining dry ingredients and beat mixture until entirely combined.

5. To assemble, scoop half the batter (approximately 1 pound) into prepared pan. Sprinkle filling evenly over batter, top with remaining batter. Spread batter out evenly with an offset spatula if necessary.

6. Bake for 21 minutes then remove from oven and sprinkle with crumble topping. Bake for another 21 minutes. Cake is done when toothpick inserted into center comes out clean.

7. Transfer pan to wire rack and let cool completely. Once cool, remove cake from outer pan. Then, by placing two large spatulas underneath cake and lifting simultaneously over mold, remove cake from inner pan. Place cake on serving platter.

Icing

1. Whisk together powdered sugar and milk until thoroughly combined. Add more powdered sugar to thicken icing - or more milk to loosen - until desired consistency is reached.

2. You can get fancy when glazing coffee cake by filling piping bag with glaze. Cut off tip of piping bag and then move your wrist in large zigzag motions from side to side in several different directions to create sophisticated designs. Or you can use a spoon to splatter, drizzle, or drench cake with glaze however you'd like!

P.S. I swear this cake is always better the next day – enjoy it as long as it lasts!

BETTY'S BUTTERMILK PANCAKES

Yield: 12 4-inch pillowly pancakes

Every Saturday morning at the bakery my team and I put together a scrumptious gluten free breakfast option for all of our customers. It wasn't meant to be a big deal; I just wanted to give those living with Celiac a safe place to eat their favorite breakfast dishes.

However, word got out and our Saturday Breakfasts began to explode! I couldn't cook 'em up fast enough and even started to gain a crowd of non-celiac folks; heck, they were just coming for some good homemade cooking!

And that's where my homemade buttermilk pancakes come in. I surely didn't think these heavenly, cake-like pillows smothered in melted butter and sugary syrup would work their way up to becoming one of our top three breakfasts but they surely did. And if you ask Betty, she would say they were hands-down #1!

Betty is actually one of the main reasons I even started selling my flour blends. Every Saturday we would make pancakes, she would politely joke about getting the recipe. One Saturday I surprised her with not only the recipe but also a bag of my Pancake Mix. As she continued coming back for more, I decided I ought to let the cat out of the bag for good. That's when I started selling not only RylieCakes Pancake Mix but our Cake Mix and Biscuit Mix too.

Before you get started on these, think a little "thank you" to Betty for her undying love of pancakes and for ever so slightly pushing me to bring my flour blends to market!

---

12 oz Pancake Mix

Preheat griddle to 350°F. Coat griddle with cooking spray before each batch.

16 oz buttermilk

1. Place Pancake Mix into large bowl and create well in center. Set aside.

2 eggs

2. Thoroughly whisk together buttermilk and eggs in 32 ounce liquid measuring cup.

3. Pour buttermilk mixture into well and then fold batter together with spatula until just combined. Batter may be slightly lumpy and this is okay – do not over mix.

4. Using ivory scoop (or 1/3-measuring cup), portion pancakes onto griddle. Cook for 3 minutes on each side. Pancakes are ready to flip when bubbles begin to rise and pop in center. Pancakes are done when both sides are light golden brown.

5. Serve warm with a pat of butter, handful of berries or nuts, dollop of whipped cream, slathering of maple syrup or all of the above!

"IT'S NOT FRUITCAKE..." FRUIT CAKE

Yield: 12 delightful slices

For Christmas last year I decided to bake for everyone rather than buy gifts. Ben wanted cinnamon rolls and chocolate chip cookies. Oma wanted a cake for all to share. My brother wanted to make sugar cookies with me. My dad asked for sea salt butterscotch cookies and I knew my cousins would kill for some caramelitas. Last but not least, I knew Ben's dad, Malone, loved fruitcake. What a great surprise this would be! My only problem was that I had never made fruitcake before...

I knew the essence of fruitcake was candied fruit, nuts, and a whole lot of booze so I decided to give it a whirl. I was absolutely stoked when my cake turned out beautifully – I was bouncing off the walls! Feeling inspired, I even made a grapefruit and bourbon simple syrup to pile on top of each slice; I thought I had hit the jackpot.

Come Christmas Eve, as we all sat around the table – stuffed from prime rib, the room lit by candles and firelight, and everyone a glass of spirits in hand – I very proudly unveiled my fruitcake in all its glory. I served everyone up a slice and anxiously awaited their feedback, especially Malone's as he was the one I made it for after all...

After a few bites the verdict was in, drum roll please...Malone said, "This is really, very good. I love it. But it's not fruitcake. It is more like fruit (insert LOOONG pause) cake." I was dying with laughter. Clearly I didn't nail it at all. Malone then explained to me what more traditional fruitcakes are like; the kind he loved to eat. Pondering over it for a second, I realized I didn't care if my cake was off the beaten path. I loved this cake. My fruit cake would simply have to be one-of-a-kind.

Cake

4 oz pecans

14.20 oz Cake Mix, divided

5.50 oz dried mangoes, roughly chopped

5.50 oz dried apricots, roughly chopped

2.50 oz dried cherries, roughly chopped

6 oz bourbon

½ tsp salt

½ tsp baking powder

½ tsp cinnamon

½ tsp ground ginger

¼ tsp baking soda

8 oz butter, softened

11.25 oz sugar

6 eggs

8.50 oz sour cream

2 oz apple juice

1 Tbsp vanilla bean paste

Grapefruit Simple Syrup

4 oz water

1 tsp vanilla bean paste

3.75 oz sugar

8 oz bourbon

1 large grapefruit, peeled and roughly chopped

QS fresh thyme

Preheat oven to 350°F. Coat 10-cup Bundt cake pan with cooking spray and set upside down on sheet of parchment until ready to use.

Cake

1. Line rimmed baking sheet with parchment, place pecans in single layer on parchment. Bake in preheated oven for 7 to 10 minutes until golden brown and have a nutty fragrance. Remove from oven, cool completely, and then roughly chop. Turn oven down to 325°F.

2. Mix chopped pecans with 1.70 ounces Cake Mix and set aside.

3. In medium bowl, combine roughly chopped dried mangoes, apricots, and cherries and pour bourbon over top. Allow fruit to soak for 30 minutes.

4. Whisk together remaining Cake Mix, salt, baking powder, cinnamon, ground ginger, and baking soda in another medium bowl. Set aside.

5. In bowl of stand mixer fitted with paddle attachment, cream butter and sugar until light and fluffy, approximately doubled in size.

6. With mixer on medium-low speed, add eggs one at a time, beating well after each addition.

7. Beat in sour cream, apple juice, and vanilla bean paste. Scrape down sides and bottom of bowl with spatula.

8. Adjust mixer to low, add dry ingredients and beat until just combined.

9. With spatula, fold in pecan mixture and soaked fruit with bourbon.

10. Pour batter into prepared pan. Bake for 60 minutes, rotating pan halfway through. Cake is done when toothpick inserted into center comes out clean.

11. Let cake cool in pan for 20 minutes before inverting.

12. Invert cake, remove pan, and let cool to room temperature on wire rack.

Grapefruit Simple Syrup

1. While cake is baking, make syrup by combining all ingredients in small saucepan with exception of grapefruit. Bring syrup to simmer over medium heat and stir gently with wooden spoon to combine. Let simmer for approximately 8 minutes until sugar dissolves and syrup thickens. Remove from heat and add grapefruit meat.

2. Using silicon pastry brush, soak cake with syrup. This can be done immediately after inverting or after cake has cooled slightly.

3. Phew, we've finally made it! Cut that beautiful cake of yours into however many slices you desire, top each with leftover grapefruit syrup, garnish with thyme, and if you're feeling it, add a dollop of whipped cream on top too!

Note: For the Bundt cake in this picture I used a Nordic Ware Vintage Star Bundt®.

PAT'S HERBY LEMON BUNDT CAKE

Yield: 10 perfectly sweet slices

I think Bundt cakes have been totally underrated for years. No one ever wanted a Bundt cake for his or her birthday, Easter, or Christmas celebration when I was growing up. And now, people are using them not only as centerpieces during the holidays but as their wedding cakes! It is fabulous - the Bundt cake is back!

If you are wondering why this is Pat's Herby Lemon Bundt Cake, it is because every time we made it at RylieCakes we would always, always, always set aside at least one slice for Pat. She would come in for no other reason other than to pick it up and enjoy.

Cake

17.50 oz Cake Mix

¾ tsp baking powder

¾ tsp baking soda

½ tsp salt

8 oz butter, softened

9.40 oz sugar

2 lemons, zested

1 Tbsp fresh thyme

3 eggs

1 egg yolk

8 oz buttermilk

1.50 oz fresh lemon juice

1 tsp almond extract

Icing

8 oz powdered sugar

2 oz fresh lemon juice

QS fresh thyme

Preheat oven to 325°F. Coat 12-cup Bundt cake pan with cooking spray and set upside down on sheet of parchment until ready to use.

Cake

1. Whisk together Cake Mix, baking powder, baking soda, and salt in medium bowl. Set aside.

2. In bowl of stand mixer fitted with paddle attachment, cream together butter and sugar until light and fluffy, approximately doubled in size. Scrape down sides and bottom of bowl.

3. Add lemon zest and thyme, beating on low speed until combined.

4. Beat in eggs and egg yolk one at a time, mixing well after each addition.

5. Add in half the dry ingredients and beat until just combined. Slowly pour in buttermilk and beat until just combined. Add remaining dry ingredients and beat until thoroughly combined.

6. Beat in lemon juice and almond extract until just combined.

7. Pour batter into prepared pan.

8. Bake for 40 minutes, rotating pan halfway through. Cake is done when a toothpick inserted into center comes out clean.

9. Let cake cool in pan for 20 minutes before inverting.

10. Invert cake, remove pan, and let cool to room temperature on wire rack.

Icing

1. While cake is cooling, prepare icing by whisking together powdered sugar and lemon juice. Add more powdered sugar to thicken icing or a little milk to loosen it.

2. To glaze Bundt cake, you can get fancy and place icing in piping bag fitted with medium plain tip. Then, pipe large circles around the top of the cake letting extra glaze drip down the sides. Or just face the facts and accept that you will be eating this cake in T minus 5 minutes and just use a spoon to drizzle (or drench) the cake with icing. Either way, don't forget to finish it off with sprinkles of fresh thyme.

Note: You can replace lemon juice and zest with orange for a fun twist on this cake. Or use rosemary instead of thyme. The citrus-herb combinations are endless here!

THE "WHAT WOULD WE DO WITHOUT WAFFLES?" WAFFLES

Yield: 5 7-inch scrumptious waffles

When I first started working on the cookbook, one of the very first things I did was pull over 100 recipes out from my binders and start to organize them into different categories. Through that process I ended up with the five chapters for this book. I decided to narrow down each chapter to approximately 15 recipes and that's when I realized, I was writing a chapter on Breakfast Bites but had no waffle recipe. What's breakfast without waffles?

I immediately called Ben and told him we were having waffles for dinner. Though confused by my formal announcement and sheer excitement, he was thrilled to have breakfast for dinner. I didn't quite nail the first batch – they were good but not great. So Ben had the pleasure of eating waffles for breakfast, lunch, and dinner until I got the recipe just right!

These waffles are ever so fluffy inside with a light crisp to their scrumptious, golden exterior. They are super easy to whip up and absolutely lip-smacking with every bite. I hope you enjoy these as much – and as often – as we do!

9.60 oz Pancake Mix

1 Tbsp cornstarch

4 tsp baking powder

¼ tsp cinnamon

¼ tsp salt

14 oz buttermilk

2 eggs

4 oz butter, melted

2 tsp vanilla extract

Preheat oven to 200°F. Place wire rack on half-sheet pan and set inside warm oven.

1. Whisk together Pancake Mix, cornstarch, baking powder, cinnamon, and salt in medium bowl. Set aside.

2. Whisk together buttermilk, eggs, melted butter, and vanilla extract in 1 quart liquid measuring cup.

3. Make well in center of dry ingredients and pour buttermilk mixture into it.

4. Fold batter together with spatula until just combined; do not over mix. There should be no dry spots left in batter but a few small lumps are okay. Let batter rest for 5 minutes on countertop while waffle iron is warming up.

5. When waffle iron is ready, coat iron with cooking spray and then using white scoop (or 1/2-measuring cup), portion batter onto waffle iron – one scoop per waffle. Close iron shut and let waffle cook for 3 minutes.

6. Transfer finished waffles to wire rack in oven to keep warm while cooking remaining batter.

7. As soon as waffles are ready, remove sheet pan from oven and start eating! Top waffles with slabs of butter, fresh fruit, toasted nuts, homemade jam (pg. #40), chocolate chips, caramel sauce (pg. #38), good ol' maple syrup, or all of the above!

Note: Waffle irons are different sizes and cook at different rates. For best results, read your iron's user manual.

SELL OUT CINNAMON ROLLS

Yield: 8 extraordinary rolls

What would Saturday mornings be without cinnamon rolls? I know – that was a loaded question. One that probably makes you wonder what you've been doing with your life to date if you haven't been wolfing down at least one cinnamon roll per Saturday.

At the bakery we made more cinnamon rolls on Saturday than anything else, and they still sold out! Every. Single. Time. Customers would become mad, sad, and miserable when they would walk up to the case and see that our cinnamon rolls were, yet again, gone.

To be honest, it usually happened in the first 30 minutes of turning on the open sign and there was nothing we could do about it. We'd have employees taking orders over the phone, regulars adding rolls to their tabs for later, and early bird customers walking out the door with full batches in hand. They were that good.

I will warn you, this recipe isn't for the faint of heart. Though, the good news is that I've seen this recipe screwed up in nearly every way possible and the end product still tasted great. Moral of the story, keep on eating until you get it right!

Pan

2 oz butter, softened

1 oz brown sugar

Filling

6 oz butter, softened

5.50 oz brown sugar

1 Tbsp cinnamon

Dough

5.50 oz Roux Mix

4.50 oz Cake Mix

1 tsp baking powder

½ tsp baking soda

1 tsp xanthan gum

1 egg

2 oz olive oil

½ tsp vanilla extract

5.50 oz milk

1 Tbsp butter

1.50 oz sugar

2¼ tsp active dry yeast

2 Tbsp Roux Mix for assembly

Frosting

3 oz butter, softened

3 oz cream cheese, softened

4.80 oz powdered sugar

1 tsp maple syrup

1 tsp salt

Preheat oven to 350°F.

Pan + Filling

1. Pan: Mix butter and brown sugar together in bottom of 9.50-inch glass pie pan. Spread out evenly and set aside.

2. Filling: Fold together butter, brown sugar, and cinnamon in small bowl until combined; set aside.

Dough

1. Whisk together Roux Mix, Cake Mix, baking powder, baking soda, and xanthan gum in medium bowl. Set aside.

2. In bowl of stand mixer fitted with paddle attachment, beat egg, olive oil, and vanilla extract until just combined. Let sit until yeast is ready.

3. Microwave milk and butter in 16 ounce liquid measuring cup to 110–115°F. Lightly whisk sugar and yeast into warmed milk and set aside to proof for 10 minutes. Mixture should rise to approximately 12 ounce mark when ready.

4. Once proofed, add yeast mixture to egg mixture and beat on low speed until incorporated.

5. Slowly add dry ingredients. Once added, adjust mixer to medium-high and beat for 2½ minutes – set a timer!

6. While dough is mixing, cover 10-by-13-inch cutting board (or larger) with plastic wrap and sprinkle with tablespoon of Roux Mix. Place dough in center of board and sprinkle with remaining tablespoon of Roux Mix. Roll out dough to 10-by-13-inch rectangle.

7. Using small offset spatula, gently spread filling mixture over dough leaving ¼-inch border around edges.

8. Start on shorter 10-inch side and roll dough into a tight, log form. Use plastic wrap to guide dough as you go. Brush off excess flour from dough with pastry brush while rolling. Use small offset spatula to help lift dough from plastic wrap if necessary. Once rolled, place in freezer for 30 minutes.

9. Remove roll from freezer and cut into 8 even slices with sharp knife. Additional Roux Mix on knife can help ensure clean cuts if dough is sticky. Roux Mix on your hands can help handle sticky dough too if needed. Freeze log another 5 to 10 minutes before cutting if dough is just too sticky.

10. Place rolls in prepared pie pan; one in center and the remaining seven encircling it. Cover with kitchen towel, place in warm spot, and let rise. Mine takes about 20 minutes when placed on top of preheated oven.

11. Bake rolls for 15 minutes and then remove from oven. Cover rolls with foil and bake for another 15 minutes until done. Rolls should be golden to dark brown on top when done and if you lift the center roll, dough should no longer look raw. Let rolls cool on wire rack until ready to frost.

Frosting

1. While rolls are baking, in mixer bowl fitted with paddle attachment, beat butter and cream cheese until thoroughly combined.

2. Add powdered sugar and beat until smooth. Beat in maple syrup and salt until just combined.

3. Spread frosting over slightly cooled cinnamon rolls with small offset spatula. Eat more than one, share only if you must, and repeat!

savory

BAKED BROCCOLI and BACON MAC + CHEESE

Yield: 6 cozy servings

At the bakery we usually sold two sizes of soup and salad: small and large. The small size was intended for lighter eaters, as a snack size, or for people who wanted to get both soup and salad. The large size was suitable as a meal for the average person's appetite. However, it was brought to my attention rather early on that when it came to mac + cheese, there was only one appropriate size: LARGE.

When RylieCakes' Front of House Manager, Kim, suggested we only serve large mac + cheese portions, I laughed out loud. She couldn't be serious, could she? Kim explained to me how it was the epitome of comfort food: warm, cheesy, easy to eat, totally filling, and only had a slight guilt factor. I'm assuming she said "slight guilt factor" rather than "full-on run you over like a freight train guilt factor" because there is broccoli in this recipe, afterall.

Kim's last point alluded to the fact that this mac + cheese also had crispy bacon… and bacon sells everything. Once she was done ranting and raving, it was clear to me why large sizes only were a must; every bite left you wanting at least one hundred more. I highly doubt you'll have leftovers, but if you do, congratulations, you have far more self-control than the rest us!

Pasta

8 oz bacon

8 oz broccoli

13 oz GF pasta elbows

5 oz sharp cheddar, grated

3 oz Gruyere cheese, grated

6 oz sharp white cheddar, grated

4 oz bleu cheese, crumbled

1 tsp pepper

¼ tsp nutmeg

2 oz butter

1.20 oz Roux Mix

24 oz whole milk

Breadcrumb Topping

5.50 oz GF bread crumbs

2 oz butter, melted

2 Tbsp minced garlic

1 Tbsp dried rosemary

Preheat oven to 325°F. Coat six 16 ounce ramekins with cooking spray.

1. Cut bacon into ¼-inch pieces. Cook in large saucepan over low heat, stirring occasionally, until bacon is crisp (approximately 7 minutes). When crisp, drain grease, set bacon bits aside, and save saucepan for step #5 (do not clean).

2. While bacon is cooking, steam broccoli by placing it in another large saucepan, filled with ½-inch water, over medium heat. Cover partially with lid and let broccoli steam for 10 to 15 minutes until tender. Remove broccoli from pan, let cool, and then chop into small, bite-size chunks. Set aside.

3. While bacon and broccoli are cooking, combine cheeses, pepper, and nutmeg in medium bowl. Set aside.

4. Bring 3 quarts of water to boil in large stockpot. Add salt until water tastes like the sea! Once boiling, add elbows and cook according to package. Elbows should be al dente when done. Strain pasta and set aside. Save 1 cup of pasta water for later use.

5. Add butter to saucepan from step #1, melt over low heat and whisk to combine with remaining bacon grease. Add Roux Mix to saucepan and cook for approximately 2 minutes, whisking constantly. Once mixture starts to brown, slowly whisk in milk. Adjust heat to medium and cook for another 4 to 6 minutes until mixture is thick and smooth.

6. Add cheese mixture to saucepan and stir over low heat with spatula until cheese is fully incorporated into sauce. Remove from heat.

7. Pour saved pasta water over elbows to loosen up. Then, add elbows, bacon, and broccoli to large saucepan with cheese sauce and stir to combine. Portion mac + cheese evenly into prepared ramekins and set aside.

8. Mix together GF breadcrumbs, butter, garlic, and rosemary in small bowl until combined; sprinkle mixture evenly over all six portions. Bake 20 minutes until breadcrumbs are golden brown. Remove from oven and let cool slightly before serving.

HOSTESS WITH THE MOSTESS CHILE CON QUESO

Yield: 2 pounds (10 addicting servings)

My family is one that often prides itself on always being the hostess with the mostess. And in order to accomplish this, you've got to make just about everything from scratch. So when my brother's girlfriend rolled in with a block of cheese spread and a can of salsa one year for our New Years Eve party, I'm quite certain we were all internally judging her just a little.

Luckily, my brother can be an ass from time to time and was the first one to give her a hard time for it – as we had all spent blood, sweat, and tears to ensure that our dish was indeed the best dish. However, as the night unfolded, my family devoured her queso dip like there was no tomorrow – my mom especially loved it. As might be expected, I accepted the challenge (that didn't actually exist…) to make the best ever chili con queso from scratch.

The next day I got to work and, to my amazement, I had everything I needed in my house. Within 30 minutes I had pulled together the most luscious, velvety cheese dip I had ever seen. And it was packed full of spicy, salty, cheesy, fresh flavors! Admittedly, Ben and I sat around with a bag of corn chips and ate nearly the entire batch. It. Was. Addicting. I hope this recipe makes it into your weekend, snack time, any time repertoire!

---

6 oz pepperjack cheese, shredded

6 oz sharp cheddar cheese, shredded

1 Tbsp cornstarch

1 oz butter

3 oz onion, finely diced

1½ Tbsp minced garlic

3 oz tomato, finely diced

1 jalapeño, deseeded and finely diced

7 oz diced green chilies

½ tsp onion powder

½ tsp cumin

½ tsp salt

½ tsp pepper

12 oz heavy cream

0.50 oz cilantro, roughly chopped

Toppings

QS tomatoes - jalapeños - cilantro - onion, sliced or diced

1. In small bowl, combine cheeses with cornstarch. Set aside.

2. In large saucepan over medium heat, melt butter; add onions and sauté until slightly golden brown.

3. Add garlic, tomato, jalapeño, and green chilies. Adjust heat to medium-high and sauté until veggies start to soften and extra liquid has evaporated.

4. Adjust heat to low and add onion powder, cumin, salt, and pepper. Sauté until spices become fragrant.

5. Pour in heavy cream and add cheese mixture to the saucepan. Stir until cheese has melted and smooth sauce forms.

6. Remove sauce from heat and add fresh cilantro, stir to combine.

7. Once sauce cools slightly, pour into serving bowl, top with whatever your heart desires, and gobble up!

SHANNON'S CHEESY BACON BITES

Yield: 48 super, duper bites

When I first went gluten free there weren't very many options on the market and the ones that did exist weren't exactly edible. They were dry, crumbly, dense, and the flavor was always a bit off. However, none of that ever stopped me from trying new gluten free products. Whenever I saw them, I bought them. I was so giddy with anticipation and full of hope – I knew something, somewhere had to be worth my while.

During a trip to the grocery store I found *Pão de Queijo* in the freezer section. It was gluten free so of course I added a bag straight to my cart. The minute I got home I preheated my oven while I unloaded my groceries. When the oven was ready, I tossed these bad boys in. Twenty minutes later, I was eating warm, chewy, cheesy bites that made my heart smile. Finally, a tasty, gluten free product!

After doing a little research on what *Pão de Queijo* actually was, I realized that they would be extremely easy to make. It was then that I started making these totally satisfying, fluffy, little bites from scratch and renamed them, Cheesy Bacon Bites.

Cheesy Bacon Bites were on the menu at the bakery from day one. They are the perfect snack suited for all ages and occasions, soak up soup better than bread itself, and always leave you wanting just one more! Shannon, our very loyal customer and friend, knew this better than anyone. Shannon's Cheesy Bacon Bites sold out every day for five years straight, but without fail, we always had a bowl set aside for Shannon.

---

2 eggs

5.50 oz olive oil

11 oz milk

5 oz sharp cheddar cheese

2 oz bacon, cooked crisp and crumbled

2 oz green onions, small diced

2 tsp salt

16.80 oz tapioca flour

Preheat oven to 350°F. Coat two 24-cavity mini muffin pans with cooking spray.

1. In food processor, pulse together eggs, olive oil, milk, cheese, bacon crumbles, green onions, and salt until well combined.

2. Add tapioca flour and pulse again until thoroughly combined.

3. Pour batter into a two-quart measuring cup. Refrigerate for 10 minutes or until ready to use.

4. Portion batter evenly among all 48 cavities; a purple scoop or tablespoon works perfect here.

5. Bake for 16 minutes, rotating pan halfway through. Cheesy bites are done when puffy and golden brown. Place pans on wire rack and let cool slightly.

6. Remove cheesy bites from pan as soon as you can and dig in! They are super duper fantastic straight out of the oven!

Note: Try replacing bacon and green onion with fillings of your choice; think chorizo, cilantro, Italian sausage, parsley, or jalapeños.

SUBLIME SOFT PRETZELS

Yield: 12 delicious pretzels

Growing up I spent a lot of time with my Oma and Opa. I could write a book just on my experiences with them – from summers in the San Juans to summers working at their company, family dinners to weekend sleepovers, running errands to all the holidays – I spent countless hours soaking in their presence.

One of the things I loved most about growing up so close with my Oma and Opa is that they always shared their German traditions with us. Oma taught me how to cook and bake German recipes, Opa told us stories of the war, and together they shared a million memories of their families and lifestyle back home. Learning about their traditions led us to create so many precious ones of our own.

One of my favorite traditions was going to Hans' Deli with Oma. Hans' was filled from wall to wall with all things German including a marvelous deli counter. And behind the deli were piles and piles of German pretzels! Their smell infiltrated the air and just one look at them made you drool. Oma always loaded up on pretzels and I always had one in my hand (mouth) when we walked out the door.

When I went gluten free I craved these pretzels more than anything! It took years to get used to leaving Hans' without one in hand. Over time I finally decided to start making my own pretzels. I can't compare them to Hans' because, well, Hans' pretzels have twenty years of memories behind them, but I can say that they will satisfy every pretzel craving you have and will leave you ready for more the minute they are gone!

Dough

11.20 oz Roux Mix

7.50 oz Cake Mix

2 Tbsp brown sugar, packed

1 Tbsp sugar

1 Tbsp active dry yeast

1 tsp salt

¾ tsp xanthan gum

½ tsp baking powder

12 oz milk, 110°F

1 egg

1.50 oz butter, softened

QS olive oil

QS Roux Mix

Water Bath

3 quarts water

3.75 oz baking soda

Topping

1.50 oz butter, melted

QS sea salt flakes

Preheat oven to 400°F. Line two half-sheet pans with silicon baking mats.

For beginners, this recipe is best done with a partner so one person can be shaping the pretzels while the other is boiling them.

1. In bowl of stand mixer fitted with paddle attachment, beat Roux Mix, Cake Mix, both sugars, active dry yeast, salt, xanthan gum, and baking powder until combined.

2. Add warm milk, egg, and butter. Beat until sticky dough forms, approximately 3 minutes on medium-high speed.

3. Place dough into lightly oiled bowl and use spatula to shape into round ball. Lightly oil top of dough and cover with kitchen towel. Place in warm spot and let rise until nearly doubled in size. Mine takes about 60 minutes when placed on top of preheated oven.

4. Ten minutes before rolling out dough, bring water to a rolling boil in 8 quart stock pot. Using a smaller pot is not advised; when baking soda is added to boiling water (step #8), water doubles in size.

5. While water is heating, place dough onto work surface lightly floured with Roux Mix. Use as little extra flour as possible; too much additional flour can compromise the texture of finished pretzels.

6. Divide dough into 12 equal parts, approximately 2.70 ounces each. Cover portioned dough with kitchen towel until ready to roll.

7. One at a time, knead portions in between palms and then roll into 14-inch ropes. Shape ropes into pretzels. To make pretzel shape, form rope into "U" shape and criss-cross sides of "U" twice. Then bring ends of dough towards bottom of "U" and seal by pressing dough together between two fingers. If dough is sticky, place some additional Roux Mix on hands.

8. Once water has reached a rolling boil, turn heat down to medium and add baking soda.

9. As soon as pretzels are formed, drop them into boiling water one at a time. Pretzels will naturally sink to bottom of pot and then float back up to surface. Once at surface, use slotted skimmer to remove pretzels from water and place on prepared pans, 6 pretzels per pan.

10. Bake pretzels for 14 minutes, rotating pan halfway through. Immediately after removing pretzels from oven, brush with melted butter and sprinkle with sea salt flakes. Pretzels are best fresh out of the oven.

JAZZED UP JALAPENO CORNBREAD MINI MUFFINS

Yield: 24 irresistible mini muffins

To be honest, I have no idea where the inspiration came to make these mini muffins. In fact, I have no recollection at all as to why we even started making them at the bakery in the first place – other than the fact that they are fabulous! And I suppose that's the only reason you need to make anything, right?!

These Jazzed Up Jalapeño Cornbread Mini Muffins check all the boxes – salty, creamy, a tad bit sweet, a little bit spicy, and topped with crisp bacon and fresh chives. You seriously cannot go wrong with such mouthwatering combinations and I swear, it is impossible to eat just one!

Batter

6.25 oz Cake Mix

4.75 oz corn flour

2 tsp baking powder

½ tsp baking soda

1 tsp salt

3 oz butter, softened

1.75 oz brown sugar

1 egg

1 egg yolk

8 oz buttermilk

2 jalapeños, deseeded and finely diced

Savory Frosting

8 oz goat cheese, softened

8 oz cream cheese, softened

3 oz whole milk

2 tsp pepper

0.50 oz fresh chives, finely chopped

Filling and Toppings

2.50 oz honey

1 lb bacon, cooked crisp and crumbled

QS fresh chives, finely chopped

Preheat oven to 350°F. Coat 24-cavity mini muffin pan with cooking spray.

Batter

1. Whisk together Cake Mix, corn flour, baking powder, baking soda, and salt in medium bowl. Set aside.

2. In bowl of stand mixer fitted with paddle attachment, cream butter and brown sugar until light and fluffy, approximately doubled in size.

3. Add egg and egg yolk one at a time, beating well after each addition.

4. Add half the dry ingredients and beat on low until just combined. Slowly pour in buttermilk and continue to beat on low until just combined. Add remaining dry ingredients and jalapeños and beat until thoroughly combined.

5. Portion batter evenly among all 24 cavities; a black scoop works perfect here. Bake for 16 minutes, rotating pan halfway through. Mini muffins should be light golden brown when done. Remove from oven and place pan on wire rack to cool.

Savory Frosting + Assembly

1. In bowl of stand mixer fitted with paddle attachment, beat together goat cheese and cream cheese on medium speed until light and fluffy.

2. Adjust mixer to low and slowly stream in milk. Add pepper and chives and beat to combine.

3. Once mini muffins have cooled to room temperature, place honey in piping bag fitted with small plain tip. Fill each mini muffin with a squeeze of honey.

4. Using purple scoop (or tablespoon), place one scoop of Savory Frosting on top of each mini muffin.

5. Place crisp bacon bits on top of frosting, pressing down slightly to flatten frosting, creating a bed for the bacon. Sprinkle fresh chives over tops of mini muffins and snack on!

YOUR FAMILY'S FAVORITE BROCCOLI BITES

Yield: 24 scrumptious bites

I hate throwing food away – absolutely loathe the idea of it. Growing up my dad was basically our trash can, he ate everything we didn't eat and whatever was leftover he made sure we ate somehow, someway. As a kid I found this pretty obnoxious; however, somewhere in the madness of growing up, I picked up my dad's habit of never, ever letting food go to waste.

One night I popped into the kitchen to see what I felt like making for dinner and found that my choices were extremely limited: broccoli or canned tuna. Since we had canned tuna the night before (don't judge), I decided I'd make something out of the broccoli. Eggs, cheese, corn chips, and onions are always staples in our house so I just had to figure out how to piece them all together.

I got after it and in just under two hours, Ben and I were lounging on the couch stuffing our faces with delightfully fried, crunchy on the outside, cheesy on the inside, slightly spicy broccoli arancini. Enjoy these as a game day snack, serve as an appetizer, or just go all in and call it dinner! Whatever you do, don't be surprised when there are no leftovers.

Batter

10.50 oz broccoli

0.75 oz fresh parsley, chopped

1.75 oz onion, finely diced

2 eggs

1 tsp pepper

½ tsp salt

1 Tbsp garlic

1 tsp Cajun spices

2.80 oz Roux Mix

2.50 corn tortilla chips, crumbed

2 oz white cheddar, shredded

3 oz Parmesan, shredded

Dredging

5.60 oz Roux Mix

2 tsp Cajun spices

½ tsp pepper

2 eggs

2 Tbsp heavy cream

Prep fryer with oil and set to 375°F. I use a Cuisinart Compact 1.1 Liter Deep Fryer. You can also heat oil in heavy skillet over stove. If using the latter method, do not heat up oil until ready to fry.

Preheat oven to 375°F.

1. Blanche broccoli. After removing from ice water, pat dry if needed, and finely dice into pea size pieces. Place into large bowl.

2. Add remaining ingredients – parsley to Parmesan – and fold together with spatula until thoroughly combined.

3. Portion batter into 24 uniform size balls; a black scoop works perfect here. Place on half-sheet pan lined with parchment and refrigerate 10 minutes. Don't worry about shape here; the batter is still too soft to form completely.

4. Remove pan from refrigerator and roll balls in between palms to form more evenly round balls. Refrigerate another 10 minutes.

5. While refrigerating, whisk together Roux Mix, Cajun spices, and pepper in medium bowl. Set aside.

6. In separate medium bowl, whisk together eggs and heavy cream.

7. Once balls are cool to touch, dredge in dry ingredients then egg mixture and again in dry ingredients. Then place balls back on sheet pan. Repeat process until all balls have been dredged. Refrigerate another 10 minutes.

8. Fry balls 3 at a time for 7 minutes per batch. Remove balls from fryer with slotted spoon and place on clean half-sheet pan lined with parchment. Keep uncooked balls in refrigerator until ready to fry. Repeat process until all balls have been fried.

9. If needed, bake balls at 375°F for 5 minutes to reheat and create crisp exteriors. Serve fresh from the fryer for best results.

Note: Keeping batter cold at all times allows for mistake-free dredging and perfectly even frying. Do not skip any refrigeration steps!

BANGING BACON BUTTER ROLLS

Yield: 8 drool-worthy rolls

When you eat gluten free on the regular, there is often something you're craving. Sometimes there are 101 million things you are simultaneously craving! Customers sent me recipes all the time of treats they wanted to see at RylieCakes. Sometimes these were family recipes, others came from Pinterest, some were ripped out of magazines, and a few copied from cookbooks. Whatever the form, I welcomed the challenge.

One day I received an email for Mushroom Pinwheel Rolls. I took a look at the recipe to find that they were just using pre-made pizza crust dough and I thought, "I can surely do this." From there, Banging Bacon Butter Rolls were born.

Just to give you an idea of how good they truly are, imagine perfectly fluffy dough rolled up with tangy cream cheese that's been infused with crispy, homemade bacon bits, mushrooms sautéed in bacon fat, and pleasantly sharp green onion morsels. All of which is then slathered in butter and freshly grated Parmesan just minutes before being removed from the oven.

If you're not drooling yet, I don't know what's wrong with you… so go on, wipe up your slobber and start making these devilishly good, one-of-a-kind, savory butter rolls!

Pan

2 oz butter, softened

1 Tbsp garlic

Filling

8 oz bacon slices

8 oz mushrooms, thinly sliced

6 oz cream cheese, softened

2 oz green onion, thinly sliced

1 tsp pepper

Dough

5.50 oz Roux Mix

4.50 oz Cake Mix

1 tsp baking powder

½ tsp baking soda

1 tsp xanthan gum

1 egg

2 oz olive oil

½ tsp vanilla extract

5.50 oz milk

1 Tbsp butter

1.50 oz sugar

2¼ tsp active dry yeast

2 Tbsp Roux Mix for assembly

Toppings

1 oz butter, melted

1 oz Parmesan, finely grated

Preheat oven to 350°F.

Pan + Filling

1. Pan: Mix butter and garlic together in bottom of 9.50-inch glass pie pan. Spread out evenly; set aside.

2. Filling: Cut bacon slices into ½-inch pieces and sauté in small frying pan until crisp. Remove from pan with slotted spoon and place bacon bits onto paper towel. Once cool, finely chop bacon with sharp knife.

3. Remove bacon grease from frying pan, leaving 3 tablespoons in pan. Place back on stove over medium-high heat and add mushrooms. Sauté until mushrooms are a light golden brown. Remove from heat.

4. Using slotted spoon, transfer sautéed mushrooms to medium bowl.

5. Add cream cheese, green onions, pepper, and chopped bacon to bowl. Fold together with spatula until fully incorporated. Set aside.

Dough

1. Whisk together Roux Mix, Cake Mix, baking powder, baking soda, and xanthan gum in medium bowl. Set aside.

2. In bowl of stand mixer fitted with paddle attachment, beat egg, olive oil, and vanilla extract until just combined. Let sit until yeast is ready.

3. Microwave milk and butter in 16 ounce liquid measuring cup to 110–115°F. Lightly whisk sugar and yeast into warmed milk and set aside to proof for 10 minutes. Mixture should rise to approximately 12 ounce mark when ready.

4. Once proofed, add yeast mixture to egg mixture and beat on low speed until incorporated.

5. Slowly add dry ingredients. Once added, adjust mixer to medium-high and beat for 2½ minutes – set a timer!

6. While dough is mixing, cover 10-by-13-inch cutting board (or larger) with plastic wrap and sprinkle with tablespoon of Roux Mix. Place dough in center of board and sprinkle with remaining tablespoon of Roux Mix. Roll out dough to a 10-by-13-inch rectangle.

7. Using small offset spatula, gently spread filling mixture over dough leaving ¼-inch border around edges.

8. Start on shorter 10-inch side and roll dough into a tight, log form. Use plastic wrap to guide dough as you go. Brush off excess flour from dough with pastry brush while rolling. Use small offset spatula to help lift dough from plastic wrap if necessary. Once rolled, place in freezer for 30 minutes.

9. Remove roll from freezer and cut into 8 even slices with sharp knife. Additional Roux Mix on knife can help ensure clean cuts if dough is slightly sticky. Roux Mix on your hands can help handle sticky dough too, if needed. Freeze the log another 5–10 minutes before cutting if just too sticky.

10. Place rolls in prepared pie pan, one in center and the remaining seven encircling it. Cover with kitchen towel, place in warm spot, and let rise. Mine takes about 20 minutes when placed on top of preheated oven.

11. Bake rolls for 20 minutes and then remove from oven. Brush rolls with melted butter and sprinkle with Parmesan. Bake for another 10 minutes. Rolls should be golden to dark brown on top when done and if you lift the center roll, dough should no longer look raw. Let rolls cool slightly on wire rack before serving warm.

BOUNTIFUL BREAKFAST BUNDT

Yield: 10 hunky servings

A few months before I closed down RylieCakes Bakery, I hired one of the best employees I ever had. Mayra was smart, funny, kind, hard working, and willing and ready to learn new things. I raved about her when given the chance, knowing she was destined for greatness.

Mayra easily transitioned from RylieCakes to the new bakery when the time came and within a matter of weeks, took over their entire savory department. I was so proud!

One morning I went in to visit and immediately noticed something unfamiliar in the case: a breakfast Bundt. What on earth was this marvelous, tasty looking creation? I asked Mayra a million questions about it – I love to know where people's inspiration comes from. And then I asked her if she would mind if I created my own breakfast Bundt for my cookbook, inspired by her of course. She said yes - obviously - with a beaming smile on her face.

This Bountiful Breakfast Bundt has everything you'd ever want in a breakfast pastry and disappears faster in my house than I could have ever imagined. I hope it gets gobbled up in your home too!

17.50 oz Cake Mix

1 Tbsp Herbes de Provence seasoning

¾ tsp baking powder

¾ tsp baking soda

½ tsp salt

1 oz olive oil

9.50 oz butter, divided

6 oz ham, medium diced

4.75 oz onion, small diced

8 oz mushrooms, thinly sliced

7 oz bell pepper, small diced

6 oz Italian sausage, cooked and crumbled

9.40 oz sugar

3 eggs

1 egg yolk

8 oz buttermilk

1 oz green hot sauce

Preheat oven to 350°F. Coat 12-cup Bundt cake pan with cooking spray and set upside down on parchment until ready to use.

1. Whisk together Cake Mix, Herbes de Provence seasoning, baking powder, baking soda, and salt in medium bowl. Set aside.

2. In medium frying pan, warm olive oil and 1.50 ounces of butter over medium heat until melted. Add ham, onion, mushrooms, and bell pepper, sauté until light golden brown. Remove from heat and stir in Italian sausage. Set aside.

3. In bowl of stand mixer fitted with paddle attachment, cream remaining butter and sugar until light and fluffy, approximately doubled in size.

4. Add eggs and egg yolk one at a time, beating well after each addition.

5. Add half the dry ingredients and beat on low speed until just combined. Slowly pour in buttermilk and hot sauce, beat again until just combined. Add remaining dry ingredients and beat until thoroughly combined. Using spatula, scrape down sides and bottom of bowl.

6. Fold in vegetable mixture with spatula.

7. Pour batter into prepared pan.

8. Bake for 45 minutes, rotating pan halfway through. Cake is done when toothpick inserted into center comes out clean.

9. Let cake cool in pan for 20 minutes before inverting.

10. Invert cake, remove pan, and let cool to room temperature on wire rack.

11. Cut into 10 slices and pair with your favorite style eggs, cups full of coffee, or even a tomato and arugula salad. Enjoy!

FANTASTIC FIGGY THYME MUFFINS

Yield: 12 stupendous muffins

Every morning at the bakery I would arrive 30 minutes to an hour before my team. I would spend that time in glorious silence creating a game plan for the day, taking into account what day of the week it was, all orders that needed to go out, any events that might be going on in the shop, and our current food supplies. I would then write everyone a to-do list for the day, marking everything that was time sensitive and allergy sensitive. I was organized, I was meticulous, and that kitchen ran like a well-oiled machine. I always put on my own list things like, "Figure out what to do with [blank]..."

This time it was figs – figure out what to do with figs. I took a look at everyone else's lists trying to pinpoint what kind of treat we needed to further fill the case. Did we need more sweet treats? More savory? In this case, we needed muffins. If you learned anything in the Breakfast Bites chapter, you cannot live without muffins.

I went to the drawing board in my brain and came up with these Fantastic Figgy Thyme Muffins. They satisfied both your sweet and savory side, were extra loaded with fillings, and smelled like a hearty, bursting herb garden when they came out of the oven. My team and I split one up into fours so we could all try a bite. All you could hear was 80s tunes jamming away in the background... we were silent – mouths stuffed, hearts smiling. A new pastry star was born.

12.50 oz Cake Mix

2 tsp baking powder

2 tsp dried thyme

½ tsp salt

10 oz sugar

2 eggs

8 oz canola oil

5.25 oz buttermilk

1 Tbsp brandy

8.50 oz sour cream

12 fresh figs

6 oz goat cheese

QS fresh rosemary

Preheat oven to 375°F. Place 12 parchment liners in standard 12-cup muffin pan.

1. Whisk together Cake Mix, baking powder, dried thyme, and salt in medium bowl. Set aside.

2. In stand mixer fitted with paddle attachment, beat sugar, eggs, oil, buttermilk, and brandy on low speed until well combined.

3. Add dry ingredients and beat until just incorporated.

4. Add sour cream and beat until combined.

5. Portion batter evenly among liners; a grey scoop works perfect here.

6. Bake for 16 minutes.

7. While muffins are baking, cut stems off figs and then quarter each only slicing halfway through – do not cut through to bottom. Stuff goat cheese into sliced figs, approximately ½ ounce per fig.

8. After 16 minutes, remove muffins from oven and place one goat cheese stuffed fig into each, pushing down slightly. Sprinkle muffins with fresh rosemary and return pan to oven. Bake muffins another 16 minutes. Muffins are done when toothpick inserted into edges comes out clean.

9. Allow muffins to cool slightly before savoring every single bite.

AWARD-WORTHY WHITE CHICKEN CHILI

Yield: 10 hearty servings

I'll be honest, when we first started making soups at the bakery my initial thought was "Really? One more thing to do everyday?" But as time went on, I found I enjoyed making soup so much that I chose to make it daily. It became a task I looked forward to.

What I loved about soups (and most savory items in general) was the ability to play around with the recipes on the spot. I thoroughly enjoyed being able to switch out ingredients to try something new, substitute ingredients when we ran out of what was needed, and add extra spices and herbs here and there to develop new flavors. It was fun, creative, and ultimately, downright delicious.

Speaking of delicious, this Award-Worthy White Chicken Chili definitely takes the cake. It was our #1 best selling soup at the bakery and I knew if the recipe were not in this cookbook, there would be angry mobs of people protesting. We wouldn't want that, now would we?

So here it is, in all its glory, the most marvelous chili of all time. And please don't forget to bake up a batch of Sweet Roasted Red Pepper Cornbread (pg. #172) to go on the side – it just wouldn't be the same without it!

Chili

1 Tbsp olive oil

1 Tbsp butter

7 oz onion, small diced

1 Tbsp minced garlic

7 oz diced green chilies

1 jalapeño, finely diced

2 tsp cumin

1 tsp paprika

½ tsp dried oregano

½ tsp coriander

¼ tsp cayenne pepper

¼ tsp salt

½ tsp pepper

24 oz chicken broth

8 oz cream cheese, cut into 16 cubes

9 oz frozen corn

30 oz white beans, drained, rinsed, and divided

3 oz water

12 oz rotisserie chicken, medium diced

1 Tbsp fresh lime juice

0.50 oz fresh cilantro, lightly chopped

1 Tbsp green hot sauce

Toppings

QS jalapeño - onion - cilantro, sliced or diced

1. Heat olive oil and butter in large stockpot.

2. When butter melts, add onion, garlic, green chilies, and jalapeño, sauté over medium-high heat for 5 minutes until onions start to turn golden brown.

3. Add spices – cumin through pepper – and sauté for another 2 minutes until spices become fragrant.

4. Add chicken broth and bring to boil. Let boil for 2 to 3 minutes.

5. Turn heat down to a low simmer and add cream cheese chunks. Stir with a wooden spoon until cream cheese is completely melted.

6. Stir in corn and 15 ounces of the white beans. Continue to simmer while preparing step #7.

7. In food processor, pulse remaining white beans with water until smooth puree forms. Add bean puree to soup and stir well.

8. Mix in rotisserie chicken, lime juice, cilantro, and green hot sauce.

9. Taste test and add further seasoning if desired.

10. Top each serving with fresh jalapeño, onions, and cilantro. Eat, enjoy, repeat!

SWEET ROASTED RED PEPPER CORNBREAD

Yield: 9 generous servings

In my world, cornbread was always a delightful side to chili, habitually served with BBQ, and never forgotten at Thanksgiving. I liked to liberally smother my cornbread in butter and then drizzle it with honey. It was what I knew and it was what I loved. It wasn't until I saw my girlfriend Kim eat cornbread for the first time that I realized I was doing it all wrong.

Kim hopped behind the bakery counter one day for lunch and served herself up a hunky piece of cornbread into a bowl. She then went over to the soup pot and ladled herself out a heaping spoonful of our Award-Worthy White Chicken Chili. To my surprise, she simply dumped the chili right over the cornbread! As she walked back to her office, I felt the need to follow her. After she sat down at her desk, she dipped her spoon into the madness and I swore I saw fireworks!

Her spoon rounded up a bite of cornbread bursting with roasted red peppers and covered in a steaming, hot, delicious mess of perfectly shredded chicken, diced green chilies, and flakes of fresh cilantro. My mouth was watering. I could not believe my eyes. How in 25 years have I never thought of this?

When making this sweet, fluffy cornbread smothered in delightfully salty, sharp cheddar cheese, remember to save at least one piece to be drenched in chili. You will surely thank yourself later!

---

5 oz Cake Mix

1.90 oz Roux Mix

2.25 oz corn flour

2 Tbsp cornstarch

2 tsp baking powder

¼ tsp salt

8 oz butter, softened

7.50 oz sugar

4 eggs

2 tsp vanilla extract

6.50 oz roasted red peppers, drained and roughly chopped

3 oz corn, frozen

3.50 oz sharp cheddar cheese, grated

Preheat oven to 350°F. Coat an 8-inch square cake pan with cooking spray and line with parchment.

1. Whisk together Cake Mix, Roux Mix, corn flour, cornstarch, baking powder, and salt in small bowl. Set aside.

2. In stand mixer fitted with paddle attachment, cream butter and sugar until light and fluffy, approximately doubled in size.

3. Add eggs one at a time, beating 30 seconds after each addition. Add vanilla extract with last egg. Using spatula, scrape sides and bottom of bowl.

4. Add dry ingredients and beat until just combined.

5. Fold in roasted red peppers and corn with spatula.

6. Pour batter into prepared pan and bake for 25 minutes.

7. Remove from oven and sprinkle cheddar cheese evenly over top. Coat sheet of foil with cooking spray and cover pan with coated side down; cooking spray will prevent cheese from sticking to foil. Bake for another 25 minutes. Cornbread is done when toothpick inserted into center comes out clean.

8. Let cool on wire rack for 15 minutes before removing cornbread from pan. Let cornbread continue to cool on wire rack until room temperature.

9. Cut into 9 large, scrumptious squares and serve with a piping hot bowl of chili.

RYLIE'S SIGNATURE SHRIMP + GRITS

Yield: 6 lip-smacking servings

I had never tried a bowl of grits before meeting Ben. In fact, I really couldn't have told you what they were exactly. What I can tell you now, is that the first time I ate grits was life changing. Ben and I had been dating for a few months and went to visit his parents for the night. I was so giddy with anticipation! Ben talked a big game about his Dad's grits and being that I live to eat, I could hardly wait to go to sleep that night just so I could wake up and try them!

The next morning was magical. Ben was right – grits really were the best ever. They were buttery, salty, creamy, and melted in your mouth. They paired well with everything on the table: bacon, fried eggs, cherry tomatoes, avocado slices, pickled jalapenos, and cottage cheese. My world would never be the same.

Since then I've made more pots of grits than I can count for breakfast, lunch, dinner, and every moment in between. I've topped them with chicken, fresh fish, fried fish, steak, bacon, chorizo, eggs, all the veggies, cheese, herbs, and more. I've even rolled, dredged, and fried them. I seriously cannot get enough of grits! I hope you get as much wear and tear out of this recipe as we do.

Shrimp

1 lb jumbo shrimp, peeled and deveined

2 Tbsp olive oil

1 Tbsp Cajun spices

2 tsp minced garlic

Grits

12 oz chili con queso

24 oz water

1 tsp salt

4.75 oz grits

2 oz heavy cream

1 oz butter

2 oz sharp cheddar cheese, shredded

1 tsp pepper

Toppings

QS tomatoes - avocado - scallions - jalapeño, sliced or diced

Preheat oven to 400°F. Line half-sheet pan with foil.

Shrimp

1. Combine jumbo shrimp, olive oil, Cajun spices, and minced garlic in large bowl and stir well. Set in refrigerator to marinate until grits are close to done. While shrimp marinate, start grits.

2. When ready, remove shrimp from bowl and place on prepared pan. Bake for 5 to 7 minutes until shrimp are pink and firm (145°F internally).

Grits + Assembly

1. Make one batch Hostess with the Mostess Chile con Queso (pg. #154). Set aside.

2. Bring water to a boil in large saucepan. Once boiling, add salt and slowly stream in grits while stirring constantly with wooden spoon. After adding all grits, turn heat down to low and let simmer, stirring occasionally.

3. Once grits start to thicken, takes 5 to 7 minutes, add heavy cream, 12 ounces chili con queso, and butter. Stir until fully incorporated. Let grits simmer for another 20 minutes to thicken. If you like thicker grits, simmer longer. If you prefer soupier grits, simmer for less time.

4. Before removing from heat, add cheese and pepper. Stir until melted and thoroughly combined. Grits should be served piping hot; as soon as they are done, dish them out!

5. Fill bowl with heaping spoonfuls of hot grits and top with succulent shrimp, fresh tomatoes, avocado, scallions, and jalapeño. Dig in and "Mmmm" like there is no tomorrow!

ALLERGY INDEX

As stated in the Allergy Guide (pg. #17), all recipes in this book are labeled for the eight major allergens, plus sugar. Each recipe states which major allergens it contains based off the products I used. Please remember to check ingredients in the products you choose to use as they may vary from mine.

In this Allergy Index, recipes are separated by the eight major allergens they are *free from*. For example, if you cannot consume dairy, simply check out the dairy free recipes list to see which recipes would be best suited for you. Page numbers follow each recipe in parenthesis. It's that easy!

DAIRY FREE RECIPES

THE BEST EVER VEGAN CHOCOLATE CHIP COOKIES (80)

BRENDA'S PEANUT BUTTER COOKIES (64)

JUST A MINUTE JAM (40)

SUNFLOWER-AGAVE GRANOLA BARS (92)

UNBEATABLE BANANADOODLES (82)

EGG FREE RECIPES

AWARD-WORTHY WHITE CHICKEN CHILI (170)

BAKED BROCCOLI AND BACON MAC + CHEESE (152)

THE BEST EVER VEGAN CHOCOLATE CHIP COOKIES (80)

CANDICE'S PB OATMEAL COOKIE SANDWICHES (86)

CLASSIC CREAM CHEESE FROSTING (36)

COULDN'T-BE-MORE-PERFECT PECAN PIE BARS (110)

HOMEMADE HONEY GRAHAM CRACKERS (84)

HOSTESS WITH THE MOSTESS CHILE CON QUESO (154)

JUST A MINUTE JAM (40)

MOM'S DARK CHOCOLATE GINGER COOKIES (62)

RYLIE'S SIGNATURE SHRIMP + GRITS (174)

SIMPLY MAGIC, MAGIC BARS (114)

SUNFLOWER-AGAVE GRANOLA BARS (92)

[TOO] SHAREABLE SHORTBREAD (70)

UNBEATABLE BANANADOODLES (82)

WOODI'S PEANUT BUTTER JELLY BARS (97)

SUGAR FREE RECIPES

AWARD-WORTHY WHITE CHICKEN CHILI (170)

BAKED BROCCOLI AND BACON MAC + CHEESE (152)

HOSTESS WITH THE MOSTESS CHILE CON QUESO (154)

RYLIE'S SIGNATURE SHRIMP + GRITS (174)

SHANNON'S CHEESY BACON BITES (156)

SUNFLOWER-AGAVE GRANOLA BARS (92)

YOUR FAMILY'S FAVORITE BROCCOLI BITES (162)

TREE NUT FREE RECIPES

ANYTHING GOES MOUSSE (41)

AWARD-WORTHY WHITE CHICKEN CHILI (170)

BAKED BROCCOLI AND BACON MAC + CHEESE (152)

BRENDA'S PEANUT BUTTER COOKIES (64)

CLASSIC CREAM CHEESE FROSTING (36)

FINGER LICKIN' LEMON CURD (46)

FOR THE LOVE OF LEMONS LEMON BARS (102)

HOSTESS WITH THE MOSTESS CHILE CON QUESO (154)

JUST A MINUTE JAM (40)

THE ONLY SWISS MERINGUE BUTTERCREAM YOU'LL EVER NEED (34)

OUT-OF-THIS-WORLD SALTED CARAMEL SAUCE (38)

RYLIE'S SIGNATURE SHRIMP + GRITS (174)

SERIOUSLY ADDICTING SEA SALT BUTTERSCOTCH COOKIES (60)

SERIOUSLY MARVELOUS BLUEBERRY MUFFINS (132)

SHANNON'S CHEESY BACON BITES (156)

SIMPLY MAGIC, MAGIC BARS (114)

SINFUL TRIPLE CHOCOLATE CARAMEL BROWNIES (94)

THE SISTERS' LAVA CAKES (47)

SUBLIME SOFT PRETZELS (157)

SUNFLOWER-AGAVE GRANOLA BARS (92)

SWEET + SALTY SPICED APPLE MUFFINS (130)

SWEET ROASTED RED PEPPER CORNBREAD (172)

SWEET, SWEET SNICKERDOODLES (72)

TANTALIZING TOFFEE CREAM CHEESE BROWNIES (104)

[TOO] SHAREABLE SHORTBREAD (70)

THE ULTIMATE PUMPKIN MUFFINS (128)

UNBEATABLE BANANADOODLES (82)

UNDERRATED WHITE CHOCOLATE CHIP MACADAMIA NUT COOKIES (66)

UNTRADITIONAL TARA-MISU (52)

THE "WHAT WOULD WE DO WITHOUT WAFFLES?" WAFFLES (146)

YOUR FAMILY'S FAVORITE BROCCOLI BITES (162)

SOY FREE RECIPES

ALL GROWN-UP ALMOND POPPYSEED MUFFINS (124)

ANYTHING GOES MOUSSE (41)

AWARD-WORTHY WHITE CHICKEN CHILI (170)

BAKED BROCCOLI AND BACON MAC + CHEESE (152)

BANGING BACON BUTTER ROLLS (164)

BELOVED BUTTERSCOTCH BLONDIES (96)

BEN'S FAVORITE CARROT CAKE (28)

THE BEST EVER VEGAN CHOCOLATE CHIP COOKIES (80)

BETTY'S BUTTERMILK PANCAKES (140)

BOUNTIFUL BREAKFAST BUNDT (166)

CLASSIC CHOCOLATE CHIP COOKIES (74)

COPY CAT GINGER BERRY BARS (116)

COULDN'T-BE-MORE-PERFECT PECAN PIE BARS (110)

DOUGY'S COCONUT PECAN FILLING (44)

FANTASTIC FIGGY THYME MUFFINS (168)

FINGER LICKIN' LEMON CURD (46)

FOR THE LOVE OF LEMONS LEMON BARS (102)

GAME CHANGING VANILLA CAKE (24)

GIGANTIC GINGER SNAPS (76)

HAMILTON HALF-MOON COOKIES (58)

"HOME IS WHERE THE HEART IS" HUMMINGBIRD CAKE (30)

HOMEMADE HONEY GRAHAM CRACKERS (84)

HOSTESS WITH THE MOSTESS CHILE CON QUESO (154)

"IT'S NOT FRUITCAKE…" FRUIT CAKE (142)

JAZZED UP JALAPENO CORNBREAD MINI MUFFINS (160)

JUST A MINUTE JAM (40)

JUST GOOD OL' FASHIONED COFFEE CAKE (138)

KATRINA'S FUDGEY OAT BARS (100)

MEGHAN'S TREMENDOUS TRIPLE CHOCOLATE BALSAMIC COOKIES (78)

MELT-IN-YOUR-MOUTH CHOCOLATE SOUR CREAM MUFFINS (126)

MOM'S DARK CHOCOLATE GINGER COOKIES (62)

NO FUSS DONUT HOLES (136)

SHELLFISH FREE RECIPES

ALL RECIPES IN THIS BOOK ARE FREE FROM SHELLFISH INGREDIENTS WITH THE EXCEPTION OF RYLIE'S SIGNATURE SHRIMP + GRITS WHICH CONTAINS SHRIMP.

FISH FREE RECIPES

ALL RECIPES IN THIS BOOK ARE FREE FROM FISH INGREDIENTS.

ACKNOWLEDGEMENTS

First and foremost, I want to thank my mom and dad. Their endless desire to help make my dreams come true is more than I could have ever asked for. I most definitely won the birth lottery and will be forever grateful.
I love you both so much more than I love cake!

To Ben, my one and only, my lobster, my soul mate, my best friend. You are my everything and nothing in this world would be worth it if I didn't have you. Thank you for always believing in me, even when I didn't believe in myself.

To Denise Firman, without your dedication to RylieCakes Bakery from day one it would have never turned into the masterpiece it was. I will never forget our seemingly endless days in the kitchen singing, dancing, laughing way too hard, and baking up a storm. Thank you for EVERYTHING, I will always value the friendship we built.

To Candice, thank you for putting up with me from start to finish on this project and for never saying no. You are beyond amazing and I hope I get the opportunity to continue working with you for years to come.

To the ENTIRE RylieCakes Bakery staff, THANK YOU! I was young when I opened the bakery and had so much to learn. Each and every one of you helped me grow and become the person I am today. I will forever hold those five years near and dear to my heart and will never forget it was all possible because of you.

To all my recipe testers and editors - Betty, Christie, Carolyn, Judy, Brenda, Austin, Donald, and Mariko - thank you for your time, energy, and endless efforts. This book would not exist without each and every one of you. Thank you from the bottom of my heart.

And finally, a huge thank you to Shivyon Mitchell for dealing with my insatiable need to perfect every last detail and most importantly, bringing my creations to life through her extraordinary photography.

Shivyon Mitchell is a wedding, travel, and food photographer based in Boise, Idaho. She is inspired by the adventurers, explorers, and seekers out there who crave a life of deeper meaning.
www.themitchellphotocollection.com.

Tara Rylie is a former bakery owner and creative entrepreneur. After five years in the restaurant space, she decided to move forward and pursue her dreams of writing a cookbook (mission accomplished if you're reading this) as well as bring her tried and true flour blends to market.

When not in the kitchen, you'll find Tara Rylie paddle boarding, hiking, traveling, kite boarding, gardening, yoga-ing, cuddling with all her pets (don't worry, there's only 21 of them), and soaking in time with her friends and family.

notes

notes

notes

notes

Printed in Canada by Friesens Corporation.

ISBN 978-0-578-47990-3

Some trademarked and/or copyrighted brands and equipment are included in this book. Mention of brands and equipment does not imply any association with or endorsement from such companies and/or owners. No association or endorsement should be inferred. Neither this book nor its author is authorized by or associated with mentioned trademarked or copyrighted brands and equipment mentioned in this book.

All efforts have been made to accurately state allergens present in each recipe. Recreating recipes at home is done at the risk of the consumer. The author cannot be held responsible for any injuries, losses, or other damages that may result from following information in this book.

www.ryliecakes.com

First Edition

ENVIRONMENTAL BENEFITS STATEMENT

RylieCakes LLC saved the following resources by printing the pages of this book on chlorine free paper made with 100% post-consumer waste.

TREES	WATER	ENERGY	SOLID WASTE	GREENHOUSE GASES
83	6,600	35	280	35,900
FULLY GROWN	GALLONS	MILLION BTUs	POUNDS	POUNDS

Environmental impact estimates were made using the Environmental Paper Network Paper Calculator 40. For more information visit www.papercalculator.org.